VEGAN FAST & EASY
COOKBOOK | by Candace Mason

111 Simply and Delicious Everyday Recipes

COPYRIGHT © CANDACE MASON, 2019
ALL RIGHTS RESERVED

No part of this publication may be reproduced, stored in a retrieval system or transmitted in any form or by any means, electronic, mechanical, photocopying, recording, scanning or otherwise, except as permitted under Section 107 or 108 of the 1976 United States Copyright Act, without the prior written permission of the copyright holder.

Limit of Liability/Disclaimer of Warranty: The author make no representations or warranties with respect to the accuracy or completeness of the contents of this work and specifically disclaim all warranties, including without limitation warranties of fitness for a particular purpose. No warranty7 may be created or extended by sales or promotional materials. The advice and strategies contained herein may not be suitable for every situation. This work is sold with the understanding that the publisher is not engaged in rendering medical, legal or other professional advice or senices. If professional assistance is required, the senices of a competent professional person should be sought. Neither the publisher nor the author shall be liable for damages arising herefrom. The fact that an individual, organization or w'ebsite is referred to in this work as a citation and/or potential source of further information does not mean that the author or the publisher endorses the information the individual, organization or website may provide or recommendations they/it may make. Further, readers should be aware that Internet websites listed in this work may have changed or disappeared between when this work was written and when it is read.

ISBN: 978-1-65861-527-3

Contents

Introduction 5

Tools for Eating Raw 7

1. Starters 9

2. Main Courses 49

3. Desserts 81

4. Sauces, Pâtés and Dips 105

5. Drinks / Smoothies 111

Measurement Conversions 114

Introduction

My name is Candace. It wasn't until 3-years ago that I truly realized, I didn't know how to take care of myself. My poor health resulted in an unhealthy mind and emotion. The best way I can describe this is by referring to zombies; whom walk around tired, sick, and unaware, searching for something I wouldn't be able to use even if I walked right into it. As many other new-to-health advocates can relate, the zombie state remained until I completely changed everything I was putting into and on my body. Most people don't or never realize the control they can have over sickness and perception of life in general. After long consideration, I became vegan with a focus on 50% raw foods. It took about 2 months to clear a lifetime of unrewarding habits, but once I started to feel more awake with a clear mind, there was no going back.

Absorbing only nature's richest and pure foods, a plant based diet opened my eyes to the opposing World I could not believe I was stuck in! A pharmaceutical pill for every emotion and feeling, products that contained more ingredients (made in laboratories) then the total years I've been alive, and diseases deliberately used to kill bacteria in processed meat and byproducts of meat. With a passion for Marketing and Research, I spent the final year of my undergraduate degree focusing in on the resistance of change within an institution or community. Discovering a raw-vegan lifestyle had such a powerful impact on my life I wanted to better understand if this case was personal, as in only applied to me, or that it was widespread throughout the World. As it turns out, there are many people who had found and followed the same path I took. The question then was; why did it take me 35 years to find it?

The core of what I learnt focused on three areas: engage, educate, and listen. Engagement allowed for me to speak and meet with many people, some who were vegan and many who had no idea what veganism was. Engagement brings together groups and communities, this helped me greatly with my research. As I was able to identify pain points within the industry, I found most of the creative Marketing for foods are of products that are not simple or pure in form. Meaning, they have been developed in labs from influences of cost and competition. Educate; I quickly discovered there were many people struggling with the same unacknowledged health problems. With so many varying messages being pushed within the market, it is no wonder people are confused. Lastly, listening and understanding the reason for resistance of change and ultimately fear within the community, I could design concepts and products that were simple in nature but effective when applied.

Tools for Eating Raw

Eating raw may seem challenging, if you've read my blog you'll find I use different types of equipment to make the most delicious meals. Each equipment is sold directly from the supplier or through Amazon. Click on the link to be lead to the same place I bought mine.

Paderno World Cuisine Spiral Vegetable Slicer:

Fancy vegetable peeling that makes eating raw easy and delicious. I like to spiral everything from zucchini to apples. This self-operating kitchen gadget is low cost with high quality. By placing your vegetables lengthwise you spin the hand toggle in clockwise motion, pushing the vegetable through to get desired shape.

Excalibur 9 Tray Food Dehydrator:

I commonly use this one to enjoy raw soup, snacks, desserts, and many other delicious meals. Excalibur offers an amazing 10 year warranty on most of their products. By getting the 9 tray, you're getting a better bang for your buck but you can certainly get one with less trays and save a little cash. My favourite recipe I use with the dehydrator is Zucchini Pizza Boats!

Hurom Titanium Slow Juicer:

I replaced my old juicer with this one recently, it's one of the better quality juicers available on the market. The Hurom slow juicer, is slow but don't let that deter you. It is a masticating juicer, meaning the way in which it extracts juice is similar to an augur, where vegetables and fruits are squeezed instead of a grinder style. This feature is what will save you from wasting a lot of juice pulp. It juices at about the rate it will take you to wash and and cut the vegetables so don't worry the 'slow' part.

Cuisinart Food Processor:

Okay, so I use this lovely piece of equipment a lot. It saves me a ton of time when chopping vegetables. Additional to creating multiple recipes, I have a full time business on my hands. This food processor is dishwasher safe, saving even more time and effort. This particular model is the 9-cup size, you can certainly buy one with less or more.

Vitamix Total Nutrition:

One of my favourite tools, the Vitamix. The Vitamix can do everything from smoothies to making soup (yes it can heat whatever your mixing). I am regularly surprised by the quality of this machine, perfect for sauces, faux cheese, and anything else you need smooth.

1. Starters

Polenta "Fries" 10
Gazpacho 11
Ajoblanco 11
Vegan Alioli Potato Salad 12
Avocado Bites 13
Chestnut and Sundried Tomato Pâté 13
Sugar Snap Pea and Mint Soup 14
Cashew Nut Cheese with Sundried Tomatoes 15
Cashew Nut Cheese with Sundried Tomatoes 15
Cauliflower Fritters 16
Chickpea Tofu 17
Cold Sweetcorn Soup 18
Mini Salad Wraps 18
Sweetcorn Fritters 19
Cous Cous Salad 20
Fideúa 21
Hummus Salad Tower 22
Leek and Potato Soup 23
Leek, Broccoli and Sundried Tomato Risotto 24
Parsnip and Fennel Soup 25
Potato Salad (No Mayo) 26
Red Cabbage Salad with Miso Dressing 27
Simple Chopped Salad 28
Spaghetti with Classic Pesto 29
Spinach, Mushroom and Coconut Pasties 30
Spinach and Mushroom Quesadillas 31
Stuffed Courgettes 32
Stuffed Mushrooms 33
Tofu with Miso and Tahini Sauce 34
White Bean Hummus with Walnuts 35
Chickpea & Cucumber Mash 36
Apple Cool Ranch Salad 37
Sweet Kale Salad 38
Pineapple Carrot Salad 38
Hearty Tomato Soup 39
Seed Flat Bread 39
Luscious Cauliflower Soup 40
Cauliflower Kale Salad with Pumpkin-Poppy Seed Dressing 41
Lemongrass Pho with Zoodles 42
Garlic Miso Zoodles 43
Spiralized Zucchini, Green Bean, Pea Salad with Parsley Salad Dressing 44
Potato and Zucchini Rosti 45
Garden Fresh Crunchy Marrow/Zucchini/Courgette Salad 46
Roasted Baby Cabbages 47
Roasted Butternut, Sage Spiral Noodles with Toasted Pecans and Cranberries 48

Polenta "Fries"

Prep+Cook Time: 30 mins

SERVES 4

1 cup cornmeal
3¼ cups water
1 tsp salt
2 tsp dried herbs of your choice (optional)
Oil for greasing

1. Grease a a dish with the oil. Mine was pyrex but it doesn't have to be heat proof as you are not going to cook it un the dish.
2. Place all the remaining ingredients in a saucepan.
3. Turn on a high heat and start to stir immediately. Keep stirring continuously. When the mixture starts to bubble turn the heat down a little. Keep stirring until you have a thick mixture which is beginning to pull away from the sides of the pan.
4. Turn the heat off and with the help of a spatula transfer the mixture to your greased dish. Use the spatula to spread the mixture evenly and level the top.
5. Leave to cool. Once it's at room temperature cover and transfer to the fridge. Leave in the fridge at least 2 hours and preferably overnight.
6. Remove from the fridge. Turn the set polenta onto a cutting board. Cut into chip sized pieces.
7. Preheat the air fryer at 390 F for three minutes. Put the "fries" into the basket and fry for about 10 minutes, until golden. You may have to do this un batches. Serve immediately.
8. Or, shallow fry in a frying pan turning to ensure they get golden on all sides. Serve immediately.

Gazpacho

Prep+Cook Time: 10 mins

SERVES 2

2 large, ripe tomatoes
3 tbsp extra virgin olive oil
1 tbsp sherry vinegar
Half a cucumber
Salt
1 clove of garlic
Half a slice of white bread with the crusts cut off and soaked in water

1. Put all the ingredients in a blender.
2. If it seems too thick (It should be drinkable) add more water.
3. Serve in a glass.

Notes:
If you wish you can put it through a strainer to make it smoother.

Ajoblanco

Prep+Cook Time: 10 mins

SERVES 6

5 oz white bread
4 cup water
1 cup of whole blanched almonds
3 cloves garlic
½ cup extra virgin olive oil
2 tbsp white wine vinegar
Salt
6 oz white grapes cut in half

1. Put all the ingredients in the blender except the water and grapes, and blend until you have a homogenous mixture.
2. Slowly add the water. Adjust salt.
3. Chill in the fridge for at least an hour. Pour into bowls. Float grapes on top of the ajoblanco.
4. Enjoy!

Vegan Alioli Potato Salad

Prep+Cook Time: 35 mins

SERVES 2

2 oz raw unsalted cashews (Soaked for at least 2 hours)
2 oz unsweetened almond milk (or other plant milk)
1 tsp white wine vinegar
Salt
1 clove of garlic
Handful of flat-leaf parsley
1 large potato

1. Wash the potato.
2. Steam or boil the potato for about 20 minutes.
3. Meanwhile prepare the "mayo". Drain and rinse the cashews. Put in a blender with the nut milk, vinegar and salt. Blend until smooth and creamy. Add more milk if necessary to achieve a mayonnaise thickness. Peel and chop the garlic clove into tiny pieces. Wash the parsley and finely chop too.
4. Stir into the cashew mixture and put in the fridge.
5. When the potato is cooked (soft all the way to the center), remove from the heat and allow to cool.
6. When the potato is cool, peel and chop into chunks about 1" square. Put in a bowl add the garlic "mayo" and stir until the potatoes are thoroughly coated.
7. Serve in small terracotta dishes and pretend you're on holiday!

Avocado Bites

Prep+Cook Time: 30 mins

SERVES 25 bites

1 cup cooked quinoa or ¾ cup uncooked quinoa
1 large avocado
1 tsp sesame seeds
Squeeze of lime juice
4 oz chopped nuts (2 oz walnuts / 2 oz brazil nuts)
Tabasco sauce to taste (optional)
Salt

1. Wash the quinoa and put in a saucepan.
2. Add three cups of water and boil for about 15 minutes or until cooked. Meanwhile mash the avocado with salt and the lime juice. It should be slightly salty because it will be diluted by the quinoa.
3. Chop the nuts. Add the tabasco to the avocado, if using.
4. When the quinoa is cooked, drain and rinse thoroughly under the cold tap. Make sure that as much water as possible is drained.
5. Mix the quinoa with the avocado mixture. With clean hands, form little balls and roll in the chopped nuts.
6. Place on a plate and chill if you're not going to eat them straight away.

Chestnut and Sundried Tomato Pâté

Prep+Cook Time: 20 mins

SERVES 4

4 oz cooked peeled chestnuts (the ones that come in a vacuum pack)
8 sundried tomatoes
2 tbsp extra virgin olive oil
Pinch of salt

1. Soak the sundried tomatoes in boiling water for 15 minutes. Drain.
2. Put all the ingredients in a blender and blend until smooth.

Sugar Snap Pea and Mint Soup

Prep+Cook Time: 25 mins

SERVES 1

**5 oz grams sugar snap peas
½ cup diced onion
5 oz grams diced potato
½ cup vegetable stock
½ cup packed fresh mint leaves
1 tsp fresh lemon juice
A little oil for saute'ing**

1. Blanch the sugar snap peas in boiling water for 30 seconds. Remove them from the boiling water and immediately put them in a bowl of iced water, to stop the cooking process. Set aside.
2. In a small pot, add the oil and sauté the onions until translucent. Add the potato and stock and reduce the heat. Allow to simmer for 10 minutes or until the potatoes are soft. Add a little water to the pot if necessary to prevent burning or sticking to the pot. Remove from the heat and place in the blender.
3. Remove the sugar snap peas from the iced water and roughly chop them up and place them into the blender with the onion and potato. Add the mint. Blend, pulse, blend until it reaches the consistency you are wanting. Add a teaspoon of fresh lemon juice and serve.
4. This soup is great at room temperature or heated up.

Cashew Nut Cheese with Sundried Tomatoes

Prep+Cook Time: 35 mins

SERVES 2

- 2 oz raw cashews, soaked (preferably overnight), drained and rinsed
- 2 tbsp lemon juice
- 1 tbsp extra virgin olive oil
- 1 tbsp water
- 6 sundried tomatoes
- 1 tsp garlic powder
- ½ tsp salt

1. Preheat the oven to 350 F.
2. Put all the ingredients for the cheese into a blender and blend for a good 5 minutes until everything is a paste.
3. Put into an oiled ramekin and bake for 30 minutes.
4. Allow to cool before taking out of the ramekin.

Cashew Nut Cheese with Sundried Tomatoes

Prep+Cook Time: 35 mins

SERVES 2

- 2 oz raw cashews, soaked (preferably overnight), drained and rinsed
- 2 tbsp lemon juice
- 1 tbsp extra virgin olive oil
- 1 tbsp water
- 6 sundried tomatoes, soaked (about 15 minutes) and drained
- 1 tsp garlic powder
- ½ tsp salt

1. Preheat the oven to 350 F.
2. Put all the ingredients for the cheese into a blender and blend for a good 5 minutes until everything is a paste.
3. Put into an oiled ramekin and bake for 30 minutes.
4. Allow to cool before taking out of the ramekin.

Cauliflower Fritters

Prep+Cook Time: 1 hour

SERVES 6 fritters

Fritters
Half a cauliflower
Half an onion
6 tablespoons wholemeal breadcrumbs
1 tsp turmeric
1tsp garlic powder
1tsp onion powder
1 tsp cajun seasoning
1 tbsp extra virgin olive oil
salt to taste

Sauce
1 plain (unsweetened) yoghurt – I used soya yoghurt
Half a clove of garlic crushed
about 1 cm of spring onion chopped fine
Handful of chopped parsley
Salt to taste

1. Put all the sauce ingredients in a bowl and mix together.
2. Put in the fridge so the flavors can develop.
3. Now remove any external leaves from the cauliflower and steam for 20 minutes until soft. While the cauliflower is cooking, chop the onion and fry in olive oil with the spices. (cajun seasoning, garlic powder, onion powder, turmeric). Once the onion is transparent, set side. Preheat the oven to 375 F.
4. When the cauliflower is cooked put it into a blender and blend until mushy. Now add all the rest of the ingredients (breadcrumbs, onion cooked with spices and salt) Blend together.
5. Place six dollops of this mixture onto a baking tray lined with parchment paper. Flatten to make patties and put in the oven for 30 minutes turning once halfway through.
6. Serve warm with the yoghurt sauce.

Chickpea Tofu

Prep+Cook Time: 15 mins

SERVES 4

1 cup chickpea flour
2 cups water
1 tsp salt
1 tsp spices (optional) for example curry powder or smoked paprika
Oil for greasing
Extra virgin olive oil

1. Grease a heatproof dish. I used pyrex. Mine measures 6 x 7 in.
2. Mix all the ingredients, except the oil together in a large nonstick frying pan or saucepan trying to eliminate any lumps.
3. Turn on the heat, I used high, and whisk constantly. The mixture will thicken and begin to bubble. Turn the heat down a little and continue whisking about 3 more minutes.
4. Using a spatula, immediately transfer the mixture to your greased dish.
5. Leave to cool. Once it's at room temperature, cover and transfer to the fridge.
6. Leave in the fridge at least 4 hours or up to overnight.
7. Remove from the fridge. Cut into bite sized pieces.
8. Fry in a small amount of extra virgin olive oil until golden on all sides. You may have to work in batches depending on the size of your frying pan.
9. Serve and enjoy!

Cold Sweetcorn Soup

Prep+Cook Time: 20 mins

SERVES 4 bowls of soup
---

2 ears of sweetcorn
2½ cup of reduced fat coconut milk
Salt to taste
Top with raw avocadoes dices with a little lime juice
Chopped tomatoes

1. Boil the sweetcorn on the cob for 10 minutes. Drain and cut the kernels off the cobs.
2. Put in a blender with coconut milk and salt and blend until completely smooth.
3. Allow to cool then put in the fridge for at least two hours.
4. Pour into bowls, taste to see if you need more salt. Top with tomatoes or avocadoes or both and serve!

Mini Salad Wraps

Prep+Cook Time: 10 mins

SERVES 2
---

4 wholewheat tortillas
Chestnut and sundried tomato pâté
1 oz spinach leaves
½ red pepper
½ avocado

1. Cut the wholewheat tortillas into strips with scissors.
2. Spread the pâté on the strips.
3. Place spinach leaves along the length of the strips. In the corner closest to you put four thin strips of pepper (about the same height as the strip of tortilla), and a slice of avocado.
4. Make a roll with the pepper and avocado in the middle.
5. You can use a toothpick to hold the roll together if you wish.

Sweetcorn Fritters

Prep+Cook Time: 20 mins

SERVES 3

Fritters:
½ cup chickpea flour
½ cup water
½ cup frozen but thawed sweetcorn
4 tbsp extra virgin olive oil (divided use)
1 generous pinch of salt

Sauce:
1 tbsp tahini
2 tbsp unsweetened plain soya yoghurt
Salt
3 tbsp water
1 tsp agave syrup or maple syrup
1 tsp garlic powder
1 tbsp capers (optional)

1. Mix the chickpea flour, water, salt and one tablespoon of olive oil in a bowl and put in the fridge at least 2 hours up to overnight.
2. Dice the capers (if using).
3. Mix all the ingredients for the sauce in a bowl and put in the fridge.
4. Take the fritter batter out of the fridge, whisk and add the sweetcorn.
5. Heat a non-stick frying pan on the stove with 1 tbsp of extra virgin olive oil.
6. Add enough batter to make a saucer-sized fritter. Fry until golden on the underside then flip until golden on the other side.
7. Remove from the frying pan and set aside.
8. Repeat until you have used all the batter adding more olive oil to the pan as necessary.
9. Serve accompanied by the sauce.

Cous Cous Salad

Prep+Cook Time: 15 mins

SERVES 4

4 oz cous cous
12 cherry tomatoes
7 oz cooked white beans

Dressing:
½ cup of extra Virgin olive oil
½ cup balsamic vinegar
1 pinch of salt
1 tsp grainy mustard
Juice of 1 mandarín orange or 3 tbsp freshly squeezed orange juice

1. Cook the cous cous according to the instructions on the packet.
2. Mix all the ingredients for the dressing together.
3. When the cous cous is cooked, pour approximately ¾ of the dressing over the cous cous and allow to cool.
4. While the cous cous is cooling wash and halve the tomatoes and drain and rinse the white beans.
5. When the cous cous is cool add the tomatoes, beans and the rest of the dressing.
6. Mix well and serve.

Fideúa

Prep+Cook Time: 30 mins

SERVES 2

4 sundried tomatoes
1 sundried pepper
1 clove of garlic
A handful of parsley leaves
2 tbsp of olive oil (extra virgin)
Half an onion
Half a courgette
Half a red pepper
6 broccoli florets
Half a teaspoon of saffron
5 oz angel hair pasta (Fideos)
Salt and pepper to taste

1. First put the sundried pepper and the sundried tomatoes in boiling water to hydrate.
2. Then dice the onion and fry it off with a pinch of sea salt. Dice the rest of the vegetables and after five minutes add them to the pan with the onion to soften.
3. Add the saffron at this point too. While the vegetables are softening, in a blender, put the now hydrated sundried tomatoes, the sundried peppers with the seeds removed, the clove of garlic, the parsley leaves and a tablespoon of olive oil. Blend together until they form a rough paste.
4. When the vegetables are soft but not too soft, (about ten minutes) add the angel hair pasta to the frying pan and move the pasta around to coat them in the vegetable juices, saffron and olive oil. Then add enough boiling water to cover the vegetables and pasta by about a centimeter. This should be boiled for about 3 minutes until the pasta seems ready.
5. Add salt and pepper if necessary. Then add the sundried tomato mixture, leave on the heat for another minute. Turn the heat off and cover everything for a few minutes more.
6. Serve and enjoy!

Hummus Salad Tower

Prep+Cook Time: 15 mins

SERVES 2

2 Beetroot (peeled and boiled/steamed)
4 oz hummus
½ grated carrot
2 oz guacamole or avocado mash*
4 whole walnuts
Extra virgin olive oil to drizzle on top

***Avocado mash:**
1 small avocado
1 pinch of salt
1 squeeze of lime or lemon juice
1 tsp extra virgin olive oil

1. First make the hummus if not using bought.
2. Make the avocado mash by mashing all the ingredients with a fork.
3. Slice the beetroot into thin slices. Start making towers. I put a beetroot slice, some hummus, some grated carrot, a little more hummus, a beetroot slice, some avocado mash, another beetroot slice, more hummus, more carrot, the last of the hummus, a beetroot slice and a little more avocado.
4. Crown with a walnut and drizzle with extra virgin olive oil.
5. Makes four towers, we ate two each.

Leek and Potato Soup

Prep+Cook Time: 40 mins

SERVES 6 bowls of soup

1 onion
2 sticks celery
4 leeks (white part only)
2 small turnips
2 small potatoes
Water
1 vegetable stock cube
1 cup almond milk
Salt
Nutmeg
1 tbsp extra virgin olive oil

1. First prepare all the vegetables. Peel and dice the onion, chop the leeks and celery into rounds, peel and dice the turnips and potatoes.
2. In a large saucepan, sauté all the vegetables in the oil with a pinch of salt except the potatoes, until starting to soften.
3. Add the potatoes and the water. You should just cover the vegetables. Add the stock cube.
4. Bring to the boil then lower the heat and let simmer for 20 minutes.
5. Remove from the heat, add the cup of almond milk and blend with a hand blender until completely smooth.
6. Taste to see if you need to add more salt.
7. Return to the heat and gently warm through.
8. Serve in bowls topped with a little grated nutmeg.

Leek, Broccoli and Sundried Tomato Risotto

Prep+Cook Time: 40 mins

SERVES 4

½ onion
1 clove of garlic
1 leek
¼ broccoli
Salt
4 sundried tomatoes
1 tbsp extra virgin olive oil
1 cup brown rice
1 vegetable stock cube
Boiling water

Optional toppings:
Parmesan cheese
Nutritional yeast
Chopped walnuts
Sunflower seeds

1. Dice the onion and garlic. Chop the leek into rounds and the broccoli into florets.
2. Sauté the onion and garlic in the oil with a pinch of salt until transparent.
3. Add the rest of the vegetables and sauté for 5 minutes.
4. Add the rice and stir in the pan for two minutes.
5. Add the boiling water and the stock cube. Enough water to cover everything in the pan by about half inch.
6. Chop the sundried tomatoes and add to the pan.
7. Cook for about 20 minutes or according to the instructions on the rice packet.
8. Whenever you see that almost all the water has evaporated add some more and give everything a stir.
9. Serve with the toppings of your choice.

Parsnip and Fennel Soup

Prep+Cook Time: 30 mins

SERVES 2

½ onion
1 medium bulb of fennel
2 large parsnips
1 vegetable stock cube
1 tbsp extra virgin olive oil
Salt
Water

1. Peel the onion and dice.
2. Lightly fry the onion in the olive oil with a pinch of salt.
3. Peel the parsnip.
4. Chop the fennel and parsnip and add to the saucepan.
5. Lightly fry for about 5 minutes.
6. Cover with water, add the stock cube, put a lid on the pan.
7. Bring to the boil, lower the heat and simmer for 20 minutes.
8. Remove from the heat and blend with a hand blender until smooth.
9. Serve in bowls topped with the leafy part from the fennel bulb.

Potato Salad (No Mayo)

Prep+Cook Time: 25 mins

SERVES 2

---

5 small potatoes
1 carrot
1 large tomato
½ spring onion
1 tsp grainy mustard
Juice of half a lemon (or 1 whole lemon)
Generous pinch sea salt
4 tbsp extra virgin olive oil

1. Scrub the potatoes. Peel the carrot ant remove the ends. Place in a large saucepan and cover with cold water. Bring to the boil then simmer for about 15 minutes or until the potatoes are soft when pierced with a knife.

2. Meanwhile, chop the tomato and spring onion.

3. Make the salad dressing. Put the mustard, lemon juice, salt and olive oil in a large bowl. Whisk until creamy.

4. Drain the potatoes and carrot. As soon as they are cool enough to handle, peel the potatoes, chop them into bite size pieces and add to the bowl with the dressing. Mix well. They should absorb more dressing as they are warm. Chop and add the carrot. Leave to cool slightly before adding the tomato and spring onion. Mix well.

5. When completely cool, cover and refrigerate at least an hour.

6. Taste the salad and add more lemon juice, oil or salt if necessary. I like a very strong lemon flavour.

7. Serve and enjoy!

Red Cabbage Salad with Miso Dressing

Prep+Cook Time: 10 mins

SERVES 2

¼ red cabbage
2 carrots
2 runner beans
¼ onion

Dressing:
1 tsp mugi miso
1 tsp whole grain mustard
1 tsp of herb infused white wine vinegar
2 tbsp extra virgin olive oil
A squeeze of lime juice
A pinch of salt

1. Mix all the dressing ingredients in a glass jar until combined.
2. Chop the cabbage, runner beans and onion.
3. Peel and grate the carrot.
4. Mix together in a large bowl.
5. Pour over the dressing and mix again.

Simple Chopped Salad

Prep+Cook Time: 15 mins

SERVES 2

8 cherry tomatoes
1 spring onion
3 tablespoons of sweetcorn (fresh or frozen)
½ large cucumber or 1 small cucumber
1 avocado
1 carrot
2 palm hearts
10 blueberries
Small handful flat-leaf parsley
3 tbsp extra virgin olive oil
1-2 tbsp balsamic vinegar
A pinch of salt

1. You're going to add all the ingredients to a large salad bowl.
2. Wash and cut the tomatoes in half.
3. Chop the spring onion into rounds.
4. Add the sweetcorn.
5. Cut the avocado in half, remove the stone, cut the avocado into chunks and peel away and discard the skin.
6. Peel and grate the carrot.
7. Peel the cucumber if the skin is tough otherwise you can leave it on. Dice.
8. Chop the palm hearts into rounds.
9. Add the blueberries.
10. Chop the parsley finely.
11. Put the last three ingredients which are for the dressing in a clean glass jar and put the lid on. Shake vigorously until well mixed. Pour over the salad. We like a strong vinegar taste so we use 2 tbsp but if you prefer a milder flavor or are not sure, start with one tbsp and see how you like it.
12. Serve.
13. Will last about 12 hours with the dressing on. If you are going to serve it later than that, keep the dressing separately but squeeze some lemon juice over the avocado just after chopping it to stop it from going brown.

Spaghetti with Classic Pesto

Prep+Cook Time: 25 mins

SERVES 2

4 oz wholewheat spaghetti
2 small potatoes
4 green french beans or a 6 courgette batons about 4 inch long (basically bean shaped)
½ oz basil leaves
2 tbsp pine nuts
½ large clove of garlic
2 tbsp nutritional yeast
3 tbsp extra virgin olive oil
Salt

1. Put a large saucepan filled with water on the stove to boil.
2. Cut the potatoes into chunks (leave the skin on) and add to the saucepan.
3. Wash the beans, top and tail them and cut them into 3 equal parts OR wash the courgette and cut it into bean sized pieces.
4. Put the basil leaves, pine nuts, garlic, a generous pinch of salt, nutritional yeast and olive oil in a blender and blend until smooth.
5. When the water is boiling add a pinch of salt, a dash of olive oil, the spaghetti and the beans or courgette. Leave to boil for 10 minutes or according to the cooking instructions for the spaghetti.
6. Place the serving dishes on the counter. Add three tablespoons of cooking water to each dish. Drain the spaghetti (and beans/courgette and potato). Put the spaghetti, beans/courgette and potatoes on the plates. Add the pesto on top and mix thoroughly. Sprinkle with more nutritional yeast if desired.

Spinach, Mushroom and Coconut Pasties

Prep+Cook Time: 1 hour

SERVES 2

1 sheet of pastry (check ingredients to make sure it's free of animal products)
½ onion
9 oz spinach
5 oz mushrooms
1 tbsp extra virgin olive oil
Cream from a 1½ cup can of coconut milk
½ tsp garlic powder
½ tsp salt
1 tbsp nut milk

1. Chop the onion and mushrooms and fry in the oil.
2. When the mushrooms are nearly cooked add the spinach. You may have to do this in stages as not all the spinach fits in the pan at once. Once the spinach has all wilted and no water is left in the pan remove from the heat and set aside to cool.
3. In a bowl mix the coconut cream with the garlic powder and salt. Preheat the oven to 390 F.
4. When the spinach mixture has cooled add the coconut cream and combine. Taste to see if you need more salt. Place the pastry on a flat surface. Roll out if necessary.
5. Cut circles of pastry using a bowl as a guide.
6. Place a few teaspoons of filling in the center of the circle, fold over and seal closed with a fork. (Or use pastry gadget). Be careful not to over fill the pasties. Place on a baking tray covered with parchment paper.
7. Make a hole in the top for the steam to escape. Brush with nut milk and bake in the oven for 25 minutes until risen and golden.

Notes:

To make coconut cream, place a can of full-fat coconut milk in the fridge overnight. Open the can and remove the part which has solidified. Save what's left (the liquid part) for use in another dish.

Spinach and Mushroom Quesadillas

Prep+Cook Time: 20 mins

SERVES 4 quesadillas

8 wholemeal wheat tortillas
1 onion
12 button mushrooms
Extra virgin olive oil
Cashew cheese
1 cups Cashew, soaked at least 2 hours
5 sundried tomatoes
A squeeze of lemon juice
A pinch of salt
Water

1. Chop the onion finely.
2. Clean and slice the mushrooms.
3. Lightly fry the onion and the mushrooms until the onion is transparent and the mushrooms are becoming golden.
4. Add the spinach one handful at a time until wilted then remove from the heat.
5. 5. Make the cashew cheese. Drain the cashews. Blend all the ingredients with ½ cup of water (preferably filtered or mineral). You should have a spreadable mixture. If it seems too thick, add more water, little by little, until you achieve the right consistency.
6. Take 2 tortillas spread 1 tablespoon of cashew cheese on each tortilla. Put ¼ of the spinach and mushroom mixture on one or the tortillas. Put the 2nd tortilla on top cheese side down.
7. Lightly fry the quesadilla in a frying pan on both sides.
8. Repeat with the rest of the tortillas.

Stuffed Courgettes

Prep+Cook Time: 1 hour

SERVES 2

2 courgettes
4 oz cooked brown rice or 2 oz raw brown rice
¼ onion
½ red pepper
1 tsp dried thyme
1 oz gound almonds
¼ oz pine nuts
½ cup vegetable stock (can be from a stock cube)
Extra virgin olive oil
Salt

1. Cook the brown rice according to packet instructions. Preheat the oven to 390 F.
2. Wash the courgettes thoroughly and cut in half. Score a line in the flesh of the courgette, leave about ½ inch border between your line and the skin. Use a teaspoon to scoop the flesh out.
3. Chop the onion and pepper. Chop the courgette flesh into small pieces. Sauté the onion, pepper and courgette with the thyme and a pinch of salt in a tablespoon of extra virgin olive oil.
4. Drain and rinse the brown rice (if using raw). Once the vegetables have softened add the rice and mix until it's taken up the flavors. Taste to see if you need to add more salt.
5. Place the courgettes in an ovenproof dish. Salt the insides (if desired). Fill the courgettes with the rice mixture using a teaspoon. Sprinkle with pine nuts and ground almonds.
6. Pour the vegetable stock into the ovenproof dish until it comes up to 1/3 of the height of the courgettes.
7. Cover and cook in the oven for 30 minutes. Uncover for the last 10 minutes so that the almond meal becomes toasted.

Stuffed Mushrooms

Prep+Cook Time: 40 mins

SERVES 4

8 large mushrooms
1 clove garlic
5 tbsp extra virgin olive oil
2 pinches of salt
1 tin flageolet beans (or any other bean you fancy)
1 onion
10 green beans
½ courgette
6 cherry tomatoes
1 tbsp sherry vinegar

1. Wash and dry the mushrooms. Finely chop a clove of garlic and mix with 3 tbsp of extra virgin olive oil. Add a pinch of salt. Break the stems off the mushrooms and set them aside.
2. Put the garlic mis in a flat bowl, add the mushrooms. Cover with clingfilm and place in the fridge overnight.
3. In the morning turn the mushrooms over.
4. Chop the onion, green beans, courgette and mushrooms stalks very finely and sauté in 1 tbsp extra virgin olive oil with a pinch of salt. Meanwhile, drain and rinse the canned beans and finely chop the cherry tomatoes. Place the beans and tomatoes in a bowl. When the sautéed vegetables are soft, set aside 5 minutes to cool a little the add to the salad.
5. Take the marinated mushrooms and grill without adding extra oil until cooked to the center.
6. Dress the salad with vinegar and 1 tbsp of extra virgin olive oil.
7. Taste to see if you need to adjust seasoning and spoon into mushrooms.

Tofu with Miso and Tahini Sauce

Prep+Cook Time: 20 mins

SERVES 2

8 oz tofu (can be plain or smoked)
4 tbsp cornflour
Salt
Extra virgin olive oil (approx 2 tbsp)
2 tbsp miso
1 heaped tbsp tahini
2 tbsp water

1. Put the cornflour on a plate and add a pinch of salt. Mix it into the corn flour.
2. Cut the tofu into batons.
3. Heat the oil in a frying pan.
4. Pass the tofu batons through the cornflour and add to the saucepan.
5. Brown the tofu batons on all sides, being careful that they don't burn.
6. While you are cooking the tofu mix the miso, tahini and water together in a bowl to form a smooth paste.
7. Remove the tofu batons from the saucepan and drain on kitchen paper.
8. Serve with the sauce on the side.

White Bean Hummus with Walnuts

Prep+Cook Time: 10 mins

SERVES 4

4 oz cooked white beans (navy beans, haricot beans, white kidney beans...)
1 tbsp tahini
Juice of ½ a lime
1 clove of garlic
Pinch of salt
1 tbsp extra virgin olive oil
2 oz walnuts
2 tbsp water
¾ oz chopped walnuts
7 green olives

1. Put the cooked white beans, tahini, lime juice, garlic, salt and extra virgin olive oil in a blender and puree until smooth.
2. In a separate bowl, blend the walnuts and water until they form a smooth paste. With a spatula mix the white bean mix with the walnut mix.
3. Chop the olives into small pieces. Add the chopped olives and chopped walnuts to the hummus.
4. Refrigerate if you have time to allow the flavors to develop.

Chickpea & Cucumber Mash

Prep+Cook Time: 20 mins

SERVES 3

- 3 cup sprouted chickpeas
- 2 small cucumbers (about ⅔ cup)
- ½ dill pickles, chopped finely
- 2 tbsp pickle juice
- 2 celery stalks, chopped finely
- ½ tsp himalayan salt
- Pinch of ground pepper
- 1-2 tbsp dijon mustard
- 1 small shallot, chopped finely
- 3 tbsp vegan mayo

1. Put chickpeas and cucumber into food processor and mix on high. Transfer into large bowl.
2. Chop pickles, celery, and shallots. Mix in remaining ingredients.
3. Serve on bed of spinach or in a wrap!

Apple Cool Ranch Salad

Prep+Cook Time: 5 mins

SERVES 2

Salad Mix:
1 green apple, thinly sliced
2 cup spring salad mix, baby greens & arugala
½ red pepper, chopped
½ cup sunflower seeds
¼ cup pecans, chopped

Cool Ranch Dressing:
½ cup vegenaise
1 tbsp almond milk
½ tsp onion powder
½ tsp garlic powder
½ tbsp apple cider vinegar
½ tsp fresh dill or touch of dried dill

1. Mix salad ingredients and set aside in medium sized bowl.
2. Using a Vitamix, mix ranch dressing until creamy smooth. Top onto salad and enjoy!

Sweet Kale Salad

Prep+Cook Time: 20 mins

SERVES 2

½ bunch of kale, finely chopped
½ orange, squeezed
1 tbsp walnut oil
1 Pear
Heritage carrots
2 tbsp sunflower seeds
½ tsp garlic powder
Pinch Thyme, dried

1. Wash and chop kale. Set aside in medium sized bowl.
2. Massage kale with walnut oil and orange.
3. Mix in other ingredients and enjoy!

Notes:
The pear was spiralized, if you don't have a Spiralizer, thin slices would also be delicious.

Pineapple Carrot Salad

Prep+Cook Time: 10 mins

SERVES 1

1 carrot
½ jicama
½ lemon, squeezed
¼ cup raisins
¼ cup pineapple
½ cup cashews, soaked
1 tbsp apple cider vinegar
1 tsp onion powder

1. Spiralize or finely chop carrot and jicama. Set aside.
2. Combine cashews with apple cider vinegar and onion powder in Vitamix, blend until smooth.
3. Mix all ingredients together and enjoy!

Hearty Tomato Soup

Prep+Cook Time: 10 mins

SERVES 4

2 roma tomatoes
½ zucchini
½ cup Kale
2 medium carrots
4 stalks of celery
¾ cup kidney beans, sprouted if you can
½ clove of garlic
¼ onion
1 cup vegetable broth
¼ tsp oregano, dried
¼ tsp basil, dried

1. Put all ingredients in Vitamix and blend until slightly smooth but still chunky. Enjoy!

Seed Flat Bread

Prep+Cook Time: 10 mins

SERVES 4

1 cup carrots, leftover juicing or finely chopped
¼ cup chia seeds
¼ cup flax seeds, ground
¼ cup sunflower seeds
¼ cup pumpkin seeds
½ cup buckwheat flour
1 cup warm water

1. After juicing, set carrots aside or finely chop carrots and use those instead.
2. Mix all ingredients together in a large mixing bowl. You should have a sticky paste.
3. Spread about a ¼ inch thick on teflon dehydrator sheets. Use a spatula to evenly mount the "dough" into large circular shapes.

Luscious Cauliflower Soup

Prep+Cook Time: 15 mins

SERVES 4

1 medium head cauliflower
2 medium sized shallots
2 medium sized carrots
2 celery stalks
1 tsp himalayan salt
1 tsp ground black pepper
1 tsp dried basil
1 tsp cayenne
1 bay leaf
1 cup finely chopped herbs (parsley, cilantro)
1 cup of pure coconut milk

1. Finely chop shallots, carrots, and celery. Put in large soup pot on stove at medium heat with bay leaf and 4 cups of vegan soup stock (homemade or cubes/dry mix).

2. Cut cauliflower florets into small chunks and set aside half. Add other half to your large soup pot on the stove. Wait 15 minutes until vegetables are soft.

3. Purée soup mixture with hand blender in soup pot or in a typical blender.

4. Put your blended mixture pack into the pot, add spices and remaining cauliflower. Cook on medium heat for 7 minutes, then add in herbs and coconut milk. If you don't care for coconut milk, use almond milk (note: it will not be as creamy; although still delicious). Wait another 5 minutes then turn off stove and wait until right temperature to serve.

Cauliflower Kale Salad with Pumpkin-Poppy Seed Dressing

Prep+Cook Time: 10 mins

SERVES 4

Salad Base:
1 cup cauliflower, finely chopped
½ cup kale, finely chopped
1 cup arugala
¼ cup raw pumpkin seeds

Dressing:
1 tbsp sesame tahnini (organic fair trade)
1 tbsp sesame seed oil
1 tbsp pumpkin seed oil, to taste
½ meyer lemon, squeezed
1 tbsp black poppy seed
1 medjool date, pitted
2 tbsp filtered water

1. Chop salad base, mix together, and set aside.
2. Put all dressing ingredients except pumpkin seed oil in a food processor of high speed blender.
3. Mix pumpkin seed oil into salad base until completely covered.
4. Add in rest of dressing, mix over lightly until ingredients are distributed evenly in the dish.

Lemongrass Pho with Zoodles

Prep+Cook Time: 10 mins

SERVES 2 bowls

1 tbsp coconut oil
1 lime, squeezed
1 lemongrass stalk, diced
½ tsp coriander
Pinch of red pepper flakes
1 tsp fresh ginger, minced
1 tsp garlic, minced
3 cup vegetable broth
2 small zucchinis, spiralized using spiralizer
Other vegetables, green onion, broccoli, snap peas

1. Heat oil in pot. Add in everything but vegetables and broth. Sauté for 5 minutes.
2. Add in broth, bring to boil.
3. Mix in vegetables and noodles, enjoy hot with extra chili flakes. Enjoy!

Garlic Miso Zoodles

Prep+Cook Time: 15 mins

SERVES 3

<u>Sauce:</u>
3 tbsp miso
1 clove of garlic
2 tbsp rice vinegar
2 tbsp tamari

<u>Zoodles:</u>
2 small zucchinis, spiralized
1 cup chick peas
Red pepper, chopped
Carrots, chopped
Handful of raw cashews
Sesame to top

1. Mix sauce in small bowl and set aside.
2. Spiralize zucchini with Spiralizer. If you don't have this equipment you can wash and thinly slice zucchini.
3. Mix all ingredients in large bowl and enjoy!

Spiralized Zucchini, Green Bean, Pea Salad with Parsley Salad Dressing

Prep+Cook Time: 20 mins

SERVES 2

2 cups spiralized zucchini/courgettes/large marrow
3 oz fine green beans
3 oz sugar snap peas

For the Salad Dressing:
½ cup tightly packed fresh parsley, chopped
2 fat garlic cloves, minced and chopped finely (about 2 tsp)
1 tsp of dijon mustard
3 tsp of freshly squeezed lemon juice
4 tbsp extra virgin olive oil
4 tbsp water
Freshly cracked salt and pepper to taste

1. Blanch the beans in boiling water for about a minute, remove immediately and place in iced cold water to prevent any further cooking to take place.
2. Then, blanch the sugar snap peas for 30 seconds, remove immediately and place in a separate bowl of ice-cold water to prevent any further cooking to take place.
3. To make the dressing:
4. Add all the dressing ingredients to a bowl and whisk until all combined. Taste.
5. To assemble the salad:
6. Place the spiralized zucchini on a salad platter.
7. Cut some of the blanched beans and sugar snap peas up and add to the zucchini. Arrange some whole beans and sugar snap peas on top. Drizzle the parsley dressing over and serve as a light meal or as a side salad.

Potato and Zucchini Rosti

Prep+Cook Time: 35 mins

SERVES 4

1 cup grated potato
1 cup grated zucchini/courgettes/large marrow
Freshly cracked salt and pepper
1 tbsp finely chopped garlic
4 tbsp finely chopped onion
Sprinkling of dried chilli flakes
Oil for frying
Roasted peppers to serve

1. Grate the potato and place in a dish towel and squeeze out any excess water. Place in a medium-sized bowl.
2. Grate the zucchini and place in the same dish towel and squeeze out any excess water. Place in the same bowl as the potato.
3. Season well with salt and pepper.
4. Place the prepared garlic and onion to the bowl with the potato and zucchini.
5. Add the chilli flakes. Stir well to combine.
6. In a medium sized skillet or frying pan, heat up some oil to cover the bottom of the pan.
7. With a tablespoon, scoop out a heaped tablespoon of the mixture. Take this tablespoon of mixture in your hands and over a bowl, squeeze. You will find there is even more water content which needs to be released, and this is from the salt, so this is okay. Once the water has been released, place the ball of potato and zucchini into the hot skillet and fry. Flatten the ball slightly and fry evenly on both sides until golden brown.
8. Eat whilst hot.

Garden Fresh Crunchy Marrow/Zucchini/Courgette Salad

Prep+Cook Time: 10 mins

SERVES 2

2 cups spiralized marrows
1 cup chopped celery
1 cup fresh basil leaves
2 cups baby spinach leaves
2 cups exotic tomatoes, chopped/halved (or cherry tomatoes)
Salt and pepper to taste
Olive oil for drizzling
Nutritional Yeast for sprinkling on the top (optional)

1. Throw spiralized marrows, chopped celery, basil and baby spinach into a bowl.
2. Add tomatoes.
3. Season.
4. Drizzle with a bit of olive oil and sprinkle with nutritional yeast.
5. Enjoy.

Roasted Baby Cabbages

Prep+Cook Time: 30 mins

SERVES 3

2 small baby cabbages
Freshly ground peppercorns
Freshly ground salt
Olive oil for basting

1. Preheat oven to 350 F.
2. Place the cabbage with the hard stem on counter top, and slice from the top to the stem, down. The cabbage will be in half now. Then cut each half again, so there are four quarters.
3. Repeat this for the other baby cabbage.
4. Baste the cut sides with a little olive oil.
5. Grind salt and pepper on the cabbage wedges.
6. Place on an oven proof dish and place in oven to cook.
7. Remove from oven, once the cabbage wedges are golden brown and crisp (about 30 minutes).

Roasted Butternut, Sage Spiral Noodles with Toasted Pecans and Cranberries

Prep+Cook Time: 25 mins

SERVES 4

Gluten-free pasta spirals

For the Butternut Sauce
A little olive oil for sautee'ing
1 cup chopped onion
1 tbsp chopped garlic clove
2 teaspoons dried sage
2 cups roasted butternut
Salt and pepper
Garnish: toasted pecans and dried cranberries

1. Cook pasta as per packet instructions.
2. In a pan with a little oil, sauté the onion and garlic for a few minutes. Then add in the roasted butternut cubes, sage and let it cook for a couple minutes until all is combined. Add to a blender and blend. Taste. Season with salt and pepper and a little more sage if necessary.
3. Place over pasta and mix through. Garnish with dry toasted pecans and dried cranberries.

2. Main Courses

Bean Ball Bowl 50
Beanburgers 51
Bolognese Burger 52
Veggieburgers 52
Chickpea and Sundried Tomato Burgers 53
Curry Bowl 54
Fruity Quinoa Salad with Tempeh 55
Homemade Vegan Kebab 56
Morrocan-Style Bean Stew with Cous Cous 57
Vegan No-Meatballs 59
One Pot "Meat" and Potatoes 60
Pasta Salad with Kiwi Dressing 61
Pasta with Sunflower Seed and Parsley Sauce 62
Roast vegetable bowl with Tofu 63
Red Peppers Stuffed with Cashew Nut Cheese 64
Red Peppers Stuffed with Tofu 65
Sweet Chilli Coriander Butternut with Almond Spaghetti 66
Tofu Beetroot Burger 67
Vegan African Peanut Stew 68
Vegan Moussaka 69
Vegetable Pasty 71
Walnut and Mushroom Bake 72
Zucchini Pizza Boats 73
Mushroom Stuffed Pizza Bites 73
Spiced Falafels On Cucumber Pasta 74
Deep Dish Pizza Pies 75
High Protein Vegetable Soup with Crunchy Golden Roasted Chickpeas 76
Green Bean and Herb Superfood Soup 77
Creamy Mushroom Garlic Basil Pesto Spaghetti 78
Roasted Butternut and Beetroot Nutty Spaghetti 79
Nutty Millet Stir Fry with Red Chilli Sauce 80

Bean Ball Bowl

Prep+Cook Time: 35 mins

SERVES 4

**14 oz cooked White beans
½ cup cooked Brown rice
3 oz Frozen Peas, defrosted
½ tsp salt
1 tsp garlic powder
4-6 carrots
1 head of cauliflower
Extra virgin olive oil
Pesto (homemade or shop bought)**

1. Prepare the pesto sauce if you are making your own.
2. Put the beans, rice, salt and garlic powder in a bowl and mash together until quite broken down almost puree like. Add the peas, and mash some more leaving some peas whole.
3. With clean hands form balls out of the mixture, about the size of a golf ball.
4. You have two options; you can cook them in the oven for 30 minutes at 390 F. Drizzle a little oil on top first and take them out when they are golden. Or shallow fry in a little oil turning them frequently until they are golden all over.
5. Meanwhile, peel and cut the carrot into sticks. Boil or steam for 10-15 minutes.
6. Make the cauliflower rice; Grate the crown of the cauliflower on a box grater until you have rice. Use the stalk in another dish.
7. Heat a little oil in a pan and add cauliflower rice and a pinch of salt. Sauté for 5 minutes.
8. Serve accompanied by the pesto.

Beanburgers

Prep+Cook Time: 40 mins

SERVES 4

3 lb tin of black beans (or red kidney beans, or cannellini beans)
¾ oz frozen peas
½ onion
½ clove of garlic
4 oz mushrooms
1 tsp mixed herbs
Salt to taste
1 tbsp extra virgin olive oil
Wholemeal breadcrumbs to coat

1. Preheat your oven to 350 F.
2. Stir-fry the onion, garlic, mushrooms and peas with a pinch of salt and the herbs for about 5 minutes or until all the liquid has evaporated.
3. Open your tin of beans, drain and rinse. Put half the beans in a blender and whizz together until they are completely mashed up. Put all the beans (mashed and non-mashed) in a bowl with the stir-fried vegetables. Mix together with a wooden spoon.
4. Check to see if you need to add more salt. Form four burger shapes, coat in the breadcrumbs (they will stick with no egg or anything, promise) and place on greaseproof paper on a baking tray.
5. Put in the oven for 30 minutes until they are warm all the way through and the crumbs are crisp but not burnt!
6. Eat hot or cold.

Bolognese Burger

Prep+Cook Time: 40 mins

SERVES 2

½ cup raw millet
½ recipe for soya (TVP) bolognese
Extra virgin olive oil

1. Cook the millet. Place in a saucepan with 1 and ½ cups of water and boil for 25 minutes.
2. Drain any excess liquid from the millet.
3. Mix with the bolognese and blend with a hand blender so that everything is well mixed.
4. Form burger shapes.
5. Lightly fry in oil until heated through in the middle and crispy on the outside.
6. Serve, if you wish in burger buns with salad and sauces of your choice.

Veggieburgers

Prep+Cook Time: 30 mins

SERVES 2

5 oz tofu
4 tbsp oats
Half a courgette, grated
1 small carrot, grated
4 tbsp soy sauce
1 clove garlic

1. Stir fry the courgette, carrots and garlic (crushed).
2. Put in a blender with all the other ingredients and blend. It should be firm enough to form burger shapes with. If not, add some more oats. Taste to see if you need to add salt.
3. Form burger shapes and if you have time, leave to chill in the fridge 30 minutes.
4. Shallow fry in a little olive oil and serve. You can enjoy these burgers on their own or with all the trimmings.

Chickpea and Sundried Tomato Burgers

Prep+Cook Time: 25 mins

SERVES 4

30g walnuts
½ large jar / 7 oz chickpeas (cooked)
2 large broccoli florets
4 sundried tomatoes
½ oz freshly grated breadcrumbs
1 tbsp tamari or soy sauce
Small pinch of salt
1 tsp garlic powder
1 tsp dried mixed herbs
Extra virgin olive oil

1. Chop the broccoli and steam it.
2. Take a large bowl, add the chickpeas and mash them.
3. Chop the walnuts and add them to the bowl with the chickpeas.
4. Chop the sundried tomatoes and add them to the bowl
5. Add the rest of the ingredients except the oil and the broccoli.
6. Take the broccoli out tof the steamer when it`s soft, chop it finely if it's not already like that and add to the bowl.
7. Mix everything thoroughly.
8. Form burger shapes with your clean hands.
9. Place in the fridge for 30 minutes to firm up a bit (if you have time)
10. Lightly fry in the oil.

Curry Bowl

Prep+Cook Time: 25 mins

SERVES 2
---

2 carrots
½ head of broccoli
2 oz farro
10 oz cooked chickpeas
½ onion
1 tbsp curry powder
1 clove garlic
2 oz raw cashew nuts
1 tbsp sesame seeds
1 tbsp extra virgin olive oil
Salt

1. Soak the cashews in water for at least 2 hours.

2. Put two saucepans filled with water on the stove to boil. Peel the carrots and cut the broccoli into florets. Once the water is boiling add the farro to one saucepan and cook for 10 minutes (or according to instructions on packet). I put a steamer over the other saucepan and steamed the broccoli and carrots. If you don't have a steamer you can boil them. Cook for 10 – 15 minutes until tender but not soggy.

3. Chop the onion and garlic quite small and stir fry in the olive oil with a pinch of salt and the tablespoon of curry powder for about 10 minutes. At this point take half the curry mixture out of the pan and set aside. Drain and rinse the chickpeas then add to the pan with the curry mixture (the half you didn't set aside), stir well for 2-3 minutes until the chickpeas have absorbed the flavor of the curry.

4. Drain and rinse the cashews. Put in a bowl and add the curried onions and garlic you set aside earlier. Blend with a hand blender until smooth you may need to add a little water, be careful not to add too much. Taste to see if you need to add more salt.

5. Now set up your bowl. A mound of vegetables, a mound of cereal, a mound of curried chickpeas. Put the curry sauce in the middle and sprinkle with sesame seeds.

Fruity Quinoa Salad with Tempeh

Prep+Cook Time: 30 mins

SERVES 2

9 oz tempeh

Quinoa Bowl:
½ cup raw quinoa
½ avocado
4 dates
½ orange
¼ salad onion
1 carrot
1 tomato
Salt

Marinade:
2 tbsp soy sauce
2 tbsp orange juice
½ tsp powdered ginger
1 tbsp concentrated apple juice

1. Mix all the ingredients of the marinade together in a bowl. Slice the tempeh. Place in the bowl with the marinade. Let marinade in the fridge for at least two hours.

2. Put the quinoa in a sieve and rinse under the cold tap. Place in a saucepan. Cover with water. Add a pinch of salt. Bring to the boil and boil for about 20 minutes. Drain, rinse under the cold tap and drain again.

3. Take a large bowl. Slice the avocado and add to the bowl. Chop the dates and add to the bowl. Chop the orange, onion and tomato and add to the bowl. Grate the carrot and add to the bowl. Also add the well-drained, cool quinoa to the bowl.

4. Take the tempeh out of the fridge. Pan fry until golden on the outside. (Both sides). Put the leftover marinade in the salad bowl and mix everything well. Check to see if you need to add more salt. Place the tempeh on top. Serve.

Homemade Vegan Kebab

Prep+Cook Time: 15 mins

SERVES 2

2 wholewheat flatbreads
Handful of mixed salad leaves
1 carrot, peeled and grated
1½ oz red cabbage, finely sliced
1 tomato, sliced
1 ball of seitan – shop-bought or homemade
1 tbsp extra virgin olive oil

Yoghurt sauce
1 soy yoghurt (unsweetened)
1 clove garlic, finely diced
1 tsp parsley, finely chopped
1 pinch of salt

1. First make the yoghurt sauce; put all the ingredients in a small bowl, mix and set aside. Cut your seitan into strips and sauté in the oil. While this is happening you need to set up the rest so you can eat it while still hot.
2. Lay out your flatbread. Add your salad ingredients – salad leaves, tomato, red cabbage and carrot.
3. Drizzle with ¼ of yoghurt sauce.
4. When the seitan in golden on the outside, take off the heat put on top of the salad, drizzle with more yoghurt sauce, roll up quickly and eat before it goes cold!

Morrocan-Style Bean Stew with Cous Cous

Prep+Cook Time: 1 hour

SERVES 4

For the stew:
1 onion
1 clove of garlic
1 slice butternut squash
1 carrot
½ courgette
1 small turnip
2-4 tsp of ras-el-hanout (according to your personal spice preferences)
A pinch of salt
2 cups cooked cannellini beans (1 large jar)
1 vegetable stock cube
water (filtered)

For the cous cous:
2 cups raw wholemeal cous cous
1 tsp salt
2 ½ cups of water
1 tbsp extra virgin olive oil

For the onions:
1 large onion
4 dates
A pinch of salt
1 tbsp balsamic vinegar
1 tbsp extra virgin olive oil

1. Peel and chop all the vegetables.
2. Sauté all the vegetables with a pinch of salt in a large saucepan for about 5 minutes.
3. Add the ras-el-hanout and stir for about two minutes.
4. Add two cups of water.
5. Drain and rinse the cannellini beans. Add to the pan. Add more water so that the beans are covered by about an inch of water.
6. Add stock cube to pan.
7. Cover and bring to the boil then reduce to a medium heat and simmer for about ½ an hour.
8. While the stew is cooking, make the onions.
9. Cut your onion in half and then into thin slices.
10. In a small frying pan, put the olive oil, the onions and a pinch of salt. You are going to leave them there for about 20 minutes stirring occasionally on a VERY LOW HEAT. You want them to caramelize but not brown.
11. Meanwhile, put the dates in a bowl and cover them with water.
12. After about twenty minutes throw the soaking water away except for about 4 tablespoons. Take the stones out of the

dates, return them to the bowl with the reserved soaking water.

13. Mash the dates and the water with a fork until you have a lumpy liquid, disgusting looking mixture.

14. Add the balsamic vinegar to the bowl and pour over the onions.

15. Evaporate the water off the onions, take the pan off the heat and set aside.

16. Now make the cous cous.

17. Put the water in a saucepan and bring to the boil.

18. When boiling add the oil and salt and then the cous cous.

19. Take off the heat, cover with a lid and set aside for 5 minutes until all the water is absorbed.

20. To serve put a layer of cous cous on the plate, add plenty of stew with plenty of the cooking liquid and top with the onions.

Vegan No-Meatballs

Prep+Cook Time: 50 mins

SERVES 2

¾ onion
1 carrot
1 tsp ras-el hanout
4 mushrooms
5 plum tomatoes
4 oz approx. vegetable stock
½ broccoli
Extra virgin olive oil
5 oz cooked lentils
4 oz cooked brown rice
1 flax egg (1 tbsp ground flax with 2tbsp of water and left to set in the fridge 15 minutes)

1. Start with the sauce. Finely chop ½ an onion and sauté in a tablespoon of olive oil. Slice the mushrooms and the tomatoes. Add to the pan with the onion. Once the mushrooms have cooked a little (about 5 minutes) add the stock and cover. Cook over a low heat for about 30 minutes. Add a little water if the sauce gets too dry.

2. Meanwhile in a saucepan, sauté ¼ of finely chopped onion. Peel and grate the carrot. Add to the pan with 1 teaspoon of ras-el-hanout and a teaspoon of salt. After about 10 minutes add the rice and lentils and allow to absorb the flavor. Remove from the heat.

3. Wash the broccoli and separate into florets. Steam for about 20 minutes or until cooked.

4. Add the flax egg to the rice and lentil mixture. Mix well. Form "meatball shapes" with your hands. Heat a tablespoon of oil in a saucepan and lightly fry the no-meatballs until slightly browned on the outside.

5. Serve the no-meatballs on a bed of tomato and mushroom sauce with the broccoli on the side.

One Pot "Meat" and Potatoes

Prep+Cook Time: 30 mins

SERVES 2

4 oz soya mince
1 large potato
1 tbsp smoked paprika
5 tbsp soy sauce
3 tbsp extra virgin olive oil
A handful of frozen peas (optional)

1. Weigh out the soya mince and put it in a bowl with the smoked paprika and the soy sauce. Stir with a spoon until well mixed then cover with water. The water should cover the mixture by about 1 inch.
2. Wash the potato and chop into large chunks.
3. In a large saucepan or deep frying pan, add the olive oil. (skip this if you want oil free or extra quick cooking) and wait until warm.
4. Add the chunks of potato and lightly fry on all sides until golden. You are not trying to fry the potatoes right through, just enough so that they hold together better in the mince.
5. Add the hydrated soy mince to the pan, and the potatoes if you didn't in steps 3 and 4, bring to the boil then turn down the heat to a simmer.
6. Simmer about 10 minutes. By the end the water should have evaporated so that there is not much liquid. If it evaporates too quickly add a little more so it doesn't burn to the bottom of the pan.
7. Add a handful of frozen peas to the pot about 3 minutes before the cooking time is up, if you wish.
8. You know it's ready when the potatoes are soft in the middle and the mince is soft.
9. Taste and adjust seasoning if necessary.
10. Serve and enjoy.

Pasta Salad with Kiwi Dressing

Prep+Cook Time: 25 mins

SERVES 2

For the salad:
4 oz wholewheat pasta (raw weight)
4 oz cooked black-eyed peas (mine were canned)
16 cherry tomatoes
2 oz watercress
¼ salad onion
1 grated carrot

For the dressing:
6 tbsp extra virgin olive oil
2 tbsp balsamic vinegar
A pinch of salt
2 kiwis

1. Put a large saucepan filled with water on the stove to boil.

2. Make the dressing. Peel the kiwis and slice into small bits. Put all the ingredients in a bowl and blend with a hand blender until smooth. Put in the fridge.

3. When the water is boiling add a pinch of salt and a teaspoon of extra virgin olive oil. Add the pasta and cook for about 10 minutes or according to the instructions on the packet.

4. Drain the pasta, put in a salad bowl, add half the dressing you made previously and leave to cool. Put in the fridge once the pasta has cooled to room temperature.

5. When the pasta is cool, it's time to set up the salad. Chop the tomatoes in half, cut the onion in rings and add to the bowl. Rinse and drain the beans and add them too. Put a handful of watercress. Peel and grate the carrot and put that on top. Add some more dressing and mix it all in so everything is coated. (Remember you might not need it all).

Pasta with Sunflower Seed and Parsley Sauce

Prep+Cook Time: 30 mins

SERVES 2

1½ cups raw sunflower seeds
3 tbsp nutritional yeast
Juice of ½ a lemon
Handful of parsley
Pinch of salt
2-4 tbsp of water
½ onion
1 spring onion
1 carrot
½ red pepper
6 broccoli florets
1 clove of garlic
Extra virgin olive oil
7 oz wholemeal spaghetti

1. Peel, wash and chop vegetables.
2. Put a large pan with water on the stove to boil.
3. Put a frying pan on the stove, add 1-2 tablespoons of extra virgin olive oil and allow to heat for 1 minute.
4. Add vegetables to frying pan, reduce to a medium heat and stir occasionally.
5. When the water in the large pan comes to a rolling boil add a little oil, a pinch of salt and the spaghetti. My spaghetti takes 8 minutes but different brands have different cooking times.
6. Put all the ingredients for the sauce (sunflower seeds through to pinch of salt) in a bowl suitable for use with a hand blender.
7. Add 2 tablespoons of pasta cooking water to the sauce and blend until smooth. You may need to add a little more to get a smooth consistency but start with 2 tablespoons and add more, little by little, if necessary.
8. Drain the pasta and put on plates.
9. Add the vegetables and top with the sauce.

Roast vegetable bowl with Tofu

Prep+Cook Time: 55 mins

SERVES 2

4 small sweet potatoes
½ courgette
½ broccoli
1 tsp dried thyme
1 tsp garlic powder
4 tbsp extra virgin olive oil
Salt
Tofu with miso and tahini sauce

1. Peel and dice the sweet potatoes.
2. Mix the olive oil, thyme, garlic powder and a pinch of salt in a bowl. Add the sweet potato and mix well.
3. Preheat the oven to 390 F. Line a baking tray with baking parchment.
4. When the oven is hot enough spread the sweet potatoes out in a single layer on the baking parchment and place in the oven.
5. Dice the courgette and cut the broccoli into florets.
6. Add to the bowl where the cubes of sweet potato were before. Mix with the left over seasoning in the bowl.
7. Once the sweet potatoes have been in the oven 15 minutes, move them around on the baking tray, then add the rest of the vegetables. Bake for 30 more minutes.
8. Make the tofu with miso and tahini sauce while your vegetables are roasting.
9. Serve the bowl of roast veg topped with tofu and the miso and tahini sauce drizzled over the tofu and the vegetables.

Red Peppers Stuffed with Cashew Nut Cheese

Prep+Cook Time: 45 mins

SERVES 2

1 large red pepper
2 oz grated courgette
1 oz grated carrot
1½ leek finely diced
2 oz raw cashews
2 tbsp lime juice
2 tbsp extra virgin olive oil
1 tbsp water
1 tsp garlic powder
½ tsp salt
1 tbsp ground almonds (optional)

1. Soak the cashews for at least 4 hours.
2. Preheat the oven to 390 F.
3. Sauté the courgette, carrot and leek in 1 tbsp of extra virgin olive oil for about 15 minutes. Meanwhile put the following ingredients in a blender; the cashews (drained), the lime juice, 1 tbsp extra virgin olive oil, the water, the garlic powder and the salt. Blend until creamy and smooth. With a spatula mix the sautéed vegetables with the cashew mixture. Taste to see if you need to add more salt.
4. Wash the pepper, cut it in half lengthwise, remove the seeds and membrane. Using the spatula put the cashew cheese and vegetable mix into the pepper, pushing it into the corners as you go.
5. Place pepper on a baking tray lined with greaseproof paper.
6. Sprinkle ground almonds on top if using. Bake in the oven for 25 minutes or until golden brown.

Red Peppers Stuffed with Tofu

Prep+Cook Time: 45 mins

SERVES 1

1 large red pepper
2 oz grated courgette
1 oz grated carrot
1½ leek finely diced
4 oz smoked tofu
2 tbsp water
2 tbsp extra virgin olive oil
1 tsp miso
½ tsp salt
1 tbsp ground almonds (optional)

1. Preheat the oven to 390 F.
2. Sauté the courgette, carrot and leek in 1 tbsp of extra virgin olive oil for about 15 minutes. Meanwhile put the following ingredients in a blender; tofu, water, 1 tbsp extra virgin olive oil, miso and salt. Blend until smooth. With a spatula mix the tofu and sautéed vegetables together.
3. Cut the red pepper in half lengthwise, remove the membrane and seeds. Put the tofu mixture in the pepper.
4. Sprinkle with ground almonds if you wish. Place on a baking tray covered with greaseproof paper.
5. Bake in the oven for 25 minutes.

Sweet Chilli Coriander Butternut with Almond Spaghetti

Prep+Cook Time: 45 mins

SERVES 4

2 large garlic cloves, chopped

2 tbsp ginger, chopped finely

40 oz butternut cubes

½ cup water (to be used to prevent the butternut from sticking)

15 oz Udon Noodles or Gluten Free Spaghetti

6 tbsp of Sweet Chilli Sauce (plus more for later!)

3 tbsp fresh lemon juice, plus extra if necessary

2 – 3 large handful of fresh coriander, chopped (stalks included)

15 oz almonds, dry toasted (plus extra if you want)

A little coconut oil for frying

1. Stir fry in a little oil the garlic, ginger and butternut cubes. add a little water to prevent sticking. Add the balance of the water. Cover the pan and let simmer for about 5 – 8 minutes. Periodically check that the butternut is not cooking too much and also check the water content. Again, if it is sticking add a little more water. The butternut needs to be a little tender at this point and not falling apart.

2. Meanwhile cook the spaghetti according to the packet instructions, and then add to the butternut in the pan with the sweet chilli sauce. Stir gently through. Add the lemon juice, coriander and almonds.

3. You may need to add a little more water to loosen it up, or you may prefer to add a little more sweet chilli sauce (I added more chilli sauce….no surprise there)

4. Stir through and serve hot with extra toasted almonds.

Tofu Beetroot Burger

Prep+Cook Time: 30 mins

SERVES 2

9 oz tofu
½ cup raw cous cous or 1 cup cooked cous cous
½ cooked beetroot
Salt
2 flax eggs (2 tablespoons of ground flax mixed with 4 tablespoons of water and left to sit in the fridge for 15 minutes).

To serve:
Bread / Burger buns
Mashed avocado

1. Cook the cous cous according to packet instructions or heat ½ cup of water in a small saucepan. When boiling add a pinch of salt and the cous cous. Cover and turn the heat off. Leave for 5 – 10 minutes until all the liquid has been absorbed and the cous cous is soft.
2. Put all the burger ingredients in a blender and blend until well mixed.
3. For burger shapes. If you have time to leave them to settle in the fridge they will hold together better. I didn't and they were still OK.
4. Lightly pan fry the burgers.
5. Serve in burger buns with some mashed avocado on top.

Vegan African Peanut Stew

Prep+Cook Time: 40 mins

SERVES 4

2 tbsp extra virgin olive oil
1 onion
2 cloves of garlic
1 tsp cumin
1 tsp ground ginger
¼ tsp hot chilli powder
1 litre vegetable stock
1 tbsp tomato puree
14 oz cooked chickpeas
1 medium sweet potato
¼ cauliflower
3 tbsp peanut butter (no added sugar)

1. Prepare the vegetables. Peel and dice the onion, the garlic and the sweet potato. Separate the cauliflower into florets.
2. In a large saucepan, add the oil and sauté the onion for about 5 minutes.
3. Add the garlic, cumin, ginger and chilli powder and keep cooking for another 1-2 minutes until the spices smell fragrant.
4. Add the stock, tomato puree, chickpeas, sweet potato and cauliflower to the pan. The stock should cover all the other ingredients by about 2 cm. If It doesn't top up with water.
5. Cover and bring to the boil then lower the heat and simmer for 15-20 minutes until the sweet potato is soft. (Check by piercing it with a knife).
6. Turn the heat off. Ladle about ⅓ of the stew into a bowl, add the peanut butter and blend until smooth with a hand blender.
7. Return to the saucepan with the rest of the stew and stir so it's well mixed.
8. Taste the stew to see if you need to add salt.
9. Warm slightly on a low heat if necessary.
10. Serve with crusty bread or a cooked grain such as rice or cous cous.

Vegan Moussaka

Prep+Cook Time: 1 hour 15 mins

SERVES 4

2 small potatoes
½ courgette
1 medium aubergine
½ onion
3 pear tomatoes
2 sundried tomatoes
1 clove garlic
1 tsp dried basil
5 oz tofu
2 tbsp extra virgin olive oil
2 tbsp white flour
1 cup unsweetened soyamilk or almond milk
4 tbsp ground almonds
2 tbsp nutritional yeast
Extra virgin olive oil
Salt

1. Start by topping and tailing the aubergine.
2. Cut it in half lengthwise and score a cris cros pattern in it. Put it in the microwave on full power for 10 minutes.
3. Preheat the oven to 390 F. Meanwhile, put the whole potatoes in a saucepan, cover with cold water and bring to the boil on the stove.
4. Boil for 20 minutes or until soft. While they are cooking chop the onion finely and shallow fry in a tablespoon of extra virgin olive oil.
5. Chop the pear tomatoes. Add the basil, garlic, tomatoes, sundried tomatoes and a pinch of salt and let cook for about 10 minutes. Take the now cooked, soft aubergine and peel. Then chop finely. Add to the tomato sauce and briefly mix. Remove from the heat and set aside.
6. Put two tablespoons of olive oil in a saucepan and heat add two tablespoons of white flour and toast the flour in the oil moving constantly with a wooden spoon. The flour should start to smell toasted but not burnt after 1-2 minutes. Then add the milk pouring it in slowly. Turn the heat down and keep moving the wooden spoon so you don´t get lumps.
7. The sauce will slowly thicken. When the sauce boils you can turn off the heat and set aside. Put the tofu in with the

bechamel and blend with a hand blender until thoroughly mixed. Salt to taste.

8. Take the boiled potatoes and cut them into slices about ½ inches thick. Brown in a frying pan in 1 tbsp of oil. Place in a layer in an oven proof dish. Take the courgette and cut rounds of about ¼ inch thick. Brown in the same frying pan. Add more oil if necessary. Layer on top of the potatoes. Sprinkle a little salt on the courgettes.

9. Put the tomato and aubergine mixture on top. Pour over the bechamel sauce. Sprinkle with ground almonds then with nutritional yeast. Cook in the oven for 30 minutes until golden on top and piping hot in the middle. If you see the top is getting too dark cover with tin foil. Serve with a simple salad.

10. Enjoy.

Vegetable Pasty

Prep+Cook Time: 1 hour

SERVES 4

1 carrot
1 small courgette
Half an onion
2 button mushrooms
1 tbsp extra virgin olive oil
Ready made pastry
2 oz cream
2 oz tomato sauce
1 tbsp almond milk
Salt to taste

1. Dice the onion, carrot, courgette and mushrooms and sauté in the oil over a low heat for about 15 minutes.

2. If your pastry is frozen take it out to defrost. Preheat the oven to 350 F.

3. Once the vegetables are lightly cooked and all liquid has evaporated from the frying pan add the tomato sauce and cream to the vegetables, stir thoroughly and heat through for about 5 minutes. Add salt to taste and remove from the heat and leave to cool.

4. Roll your pastry into a rectangle if necessary, place on a flat surface. Cover half the pastry with the vegetable filling. Fold the pastry closed and seal with a fork.

5. Brush the pastry with almond milk and make some holes in the top for steam to escape.

6. Cook in the oven for 30 minutes or until golden brown.

Walnut and Mushroom Bake

Prep+Cook Time: 1 hour

SERVES 2

1 small onion
8 oz mushrooms
2 oz walnuts
1 tbsp extra virgin olive oil
2 oz wholemeal breadcrumbs
2 tbsp chopped parsley
Salt and pepper
1 packet of puff pastry or filo pastry
Melted (vegan) butter (if using filo pastry) or 4 oz ml soya milk if using puff pastry

1. Chop onion, mushrooms and walnuts finely.
2. Sauté onions, mushrooms and walnuts in oil for about 5 minutes.
3. Transfer to a bowl, And leave to cool 10 minutes.
4. Add breadcrumbs, parsley, salt and pepper and mix well. Allow to cool completely.
5. If using puff pastry: put the pastry on a piece of baking paper on a baking tray, put the filling on half of the pastry, leaving a ½ inches space at the edge. Fold the top down over the filling and seal the edges with a fork. Make a couple of slits in the top for the steam to escape. Brush with soy milk.
6. Bake in the oven at 390 F for approx 30 minutes until the pastry has puffed up, is golden on top and the filling is piping hot all the way through.
7. If using filo pastry: put a piece of baking paper on a baking tray. Melt the (vegan) butter/margarine in a small saucepan and remove from the heat. Take a sheet of filo pastry and brush with the melted butter. Add five more layers brushing each one with melted butter.
8. Put the filling un the center of the pastry. Cover the filling with the pastry. Adding melted butter to the layers as you go. You want to make the shape of a bag.
9. Cook in the oven at 420 F for 30 minutes.

Zucchini Pizza Boats

Prep+Cook Time: 1 hour

SERVES 2

2 small zucchinis, halved lengthwise
4 tbsp organic pizza sauce
¼ onion, chopped
½ tomato, chopped
Olives
Tuscan kale, chopped
1 mushroom, sliced
Pinch of dried thyme, on each boat

1. Wash and prep vegetables.
2. Cut zucchinis in half lengthwise. In this case it is not necessarily a boat, because we did not scoop out the inside of the zucchini. If you would prefer, scoop the zucchini about ½ way then mix in zucchini leftover with other ingredients.
3. Place pizza sauce on zucchini inside and then top with other vegetables.
4. Season with thyme. Place on mesh tray and put in dehydrator for 1.5 hours at 245 F. If you don't have time and just want a quick snack, either enjoy non-dehydrated or bake in oven at 550 F for 20 minutes.

Mushroom Stuffed Pizza Bites

Prep+Cook Time: 1 hour 20 mins

SERVES 10 bites

12 mushrooms
1 cup spinach or kale
½ shallot
2 roma tomatoes
1 tsp thyme, dried
1 tsp basil, dried
Organic marinara or pizza sauce

1. After washing vegetables, using a knife carefully remove stem base of mushrooms, leaving them in a bowl shape. Set Aside.
2. Put spinach, shallot, tomatoes, thyme, basil, and leftover from mushroom into food processor and chop until chunky.
3. Put Marinara or pizza sauce onto bottom of mushrooms where you have created your bowl shape. Then pile vegetable topping and place on mesh dehydrator tray.
4. Put in dehydrator and dry at 250 F for 1 hour or until reached desired moisture.

Fresh parsley to garnish

Spiced Falafels On Cucumber Pasta

Prep+Cook Time: 2 hours 50 mins

SERVES 8 balls

½ cup hemp seeds
1 cup chick peas, sprouted (raw) or organic canned (not raw)
½ lemon, squeezed
2 tbsp olive oil
1 garlic clove (It will be raw so do ½ if you want less intensity)
1 tsp cumin
¼ tsp cayenne
Pinch of ground cardamom
1 tsp onion powder
¼ cup parsley
Sesame seeds

1. Put all ingredients in food processor and mix on high until fully combined. Transfer to large bowl.
2. Chop parsley in food processor then add to falafel mix.
3. Roll mixture into 10 – 12 balls and roll in sesame seeds. Place on mesh dehydrator tray and using a dehydrator, dry at 250 F for 2.5 hours.
4. Using a Spiralizer, spiralize 2 cucumbers into pasta style. Transfer onto a plate and soak up water with clean tea towel.
5. Once dehydrated, remove falafels and top on cucumber. Add sauce below if you wish.

Deep Dish Pizza Pies

Prep+Cook Time: 3 hours 50 mins

SERVES 2

Crust:
1 cup almonds
1 cup pumpkin seeds
1 red bell pepper
1 large garlic clove
1 shallot
2 tbsp coconut nectar
Sea salt
Ground pepper

Topping:
Organic pizza sauce
Homemade hummus
Mushrooms
Fresh basil
Yellow pepper
Dried oregano

1. Put almonds and pumpkin seeds in food processor and mix until larger then grain of sand.
2. Add in other crust ingredients and pulse until fully mixed.
3. Make crust into large balls then flatten to about a ½ inch each.
4. Press lightly into center of crust to create a bowl-like shape.
5. Top pizza with ingredients.
6. Place pies on mesh dehydrator tray.
7. Using a dehydrator, dry at 250 F for 3-4 hours, or until you've reached desired moisture, then enjoy!

High Protein Vegetable Soup with Crunchy Golden Roasted Chickpeas

Prep+Cook Time: 45 mins

SERVES 9

A little oil for saute'ing
1 cup chopped onion
1 cup chopped green pepper
6 long celery stalks and tops, chopped
2 ½ cups chopped carrots
2 large zucchini's, chopped
2 cups cooked chickpeas
Salt and pepper to taste
Dried oregano
2 cups vegetable stock

1. In a large pot, and on medium heat, sauté the onions until just translucent. Add the green pepper, celery and celery tops. Stir around for about a minute and then add the carrots, zucchini's, chickpeas, oregano and stock. Bring to the boil, stirring occasionally and then reduce the temperature to simmer with the lid on the pot. Let simmer for about 20 minutes or until the vegetables have softened. Taste.

2. Season with salt and pepper. Add more oregano if you feel it is needed. Taste.

3. Add the vegetables to the blender. Blend until the vegetables reach the consistency you want.

4. Serve hot and with some crunchy roasted chickpeas.

5. Enjoy.

Green Bean and Herb Superfood Soup

Prep+Cook Time: 20 mins

SERVES 2

10 oz green beans, chopped
1 medium sized onion, chopped
1 cup vegetable stock
2 fresh rosemary stalks
Handful of fresh basil
Salt and pepper to taste
¼ tsp of spirulina powder
Chia seeds for topping

1. In a medium sized pot, on medium heat sauté onion.
2. Add beans, stock and herbs (leaving the leaves of the rosemary on the stalk, they will fall off whilst cooking)
3. Cook until the beans are tender about 5-7 minutes.
4. Remove the rosemary stalks and throw them away.
5. Add the pot contents to a blender, and blend until smooth.
6. Taste, and see if anymore salt or pepper is needed.
7. Add spirulina. Give it a quick blitz. Place into soup bowls. Top with chia.
8. Enjoy.

Creamy Mushroom Garlic Basil Pesto Spaghetti

Prep+Cook Time: 20 mins

SERVES 4

Gluten-free spaghetti
2 cloves garlic, chopped
10 oz mushrooms, sliced
A little butter for the mushrooms

For the pesto sauce:
4 oz butter
2 oz gluten-free all purpose flour
3 cups almond milk
10 oz basil pesto
Salt and pepper if needed

1. Cook spaghetti as per packet instructions.
2. In another pot, on medium heat, add butter and sauté the sliced mushrooms and garlic. Set aside once done. In the same pot you used for the mushrooms add the butter for the sauce, allow to bubble and boil slightly. Remove from the heat and add in the flour. Stir well. Return to the heat and stir well adding the milk in gradually. This could be a bit of an arm workout, but it is nothing serious. Keep on stirring until the sauce thickens and the milk is finished. Add the pesto, most of the mushrooms and stir. Take the pot off the stove.
3. On individual plates, serve the pesto sauce on top of the spaghetti and top with the balance of the mushrooms.
4. Enjoy.

Roasted Butternut and Beetroot Nutty Spaghetti

Prep+Cook Time: 30 mins

SERVES 4

Gluten-free spaghetti
2 cups grated raw butternut
½ cup grated raw beetroot
Salt and pepper to taste
A drizzling of extra virgin olive oil for the roasting of the vegetables
A little butter or oil for cooking the garlic, sage and onions
4 garlic cloves, finely chopped
Handful of fresh sage leaves
6 spring onions, finely chopped

To serve with:
freshly squeezed lemon juice
toasted almonds, chopped
toasted pumpkin seeds

1. Preheat oven to 350 F.
2. Grate the butternut and beetroot.
3. Place on a baking tray with a little oil, salt and pepper. Place in a preheated oven and roast for about 10 minutes. After about 5 minutes, give the vegetables a stir.
4. Whilst the vegetables are roasting, cook up the spaghetti.
5. Once the vegetables are done, remove from the oven.
6. In the meanwhile, heat up a little oil in a pan and cook the garlic and sage for a couple of minutes, lastly add the spring onions and give them a stir.
7. Then add the cooked spaghetti, and quickly toss in the roasted butternut and beetroot. You may find that the spaghetti starts turning a bit pink from the beetroot, don't worry it is fine. Give this meal a squeeze of lemon juice and top with toasted almonds and toasted pumpkin seeds.

Nutty Millet Stir Fry with Red Chilli Sauce

Prep+Cook Time: 20 mins

SERVES 4

For the sauce:
2 ½ tbsp of red chilli soy sauce
2 ½ tbsp of honey
Zest and juice of one large lemon

For the stir-fry:
⅔ cups sliced white onion
⅞ cups sliced yellow pepper
2 cups sliced red/purple cabbage
4 cups carrot
1 cup snap peas, roughly chopped
A little olive oil for frying
1 cup cooked millet
¾ cup dry toasted almonds

1. For the sauce: Mix the soy, honey and zest together in a small pot. Add about half of the lemon juice and taste. If you feel it needs a bit more of a tarty taste, then add the rest. I generally end up using juice from a whole lemon. Set aside to be heated up just before serving.

2. On medium heat, add the oil in either a large frying pan or wok. Once heated add the carrots first and give them a head start for a couple seconds, (as they are the hardest raw vegetable) then add the onion, pepper, snap peas and lastly the red/purple cabbage. Stir continuously just for a few minutes until just lightly cooked, but still crunchy.

3. Add the cooked millet, stir around well and let it nestle around nicely among the veggies. (Now this is the time to multi-task, while you are stirring around the millet, heat up the sauce.

4. Serve hot and add the dry toasted almonds separately. I prefer to do this to extend the crunch factor.

3. Desserts

Vegan Chocolate Banana Pie **82**
Vegan Chocolate Orange Pie **83**
Chocolate and Strawberry Cup **84**
Fruit 'n' Nut Balls **85**
Homemade Chocolate Spread **86**
Mint Basil Choc Chip Ice-Cream **86**
Peanut Butter Truffles **87**
Piña Colada Chia Seed Mousse **87**
Valentine's Day Truffles **88**
Vegan Mint Chocolate Thins **89**
Almond Biscuits **90**
Melting Blueberry Fudge **90**
Quinoa, Carrot and Baby Marrow Cakes **91**
Vegan Opera Slice **92**
Strawberry Chocolate Vegan Cheesecake **94**
Brownie With Avocado Choco Icing & Kiwi Gummies **96**
Choco Chip Cookie Bites **97**
Apple Stacks with Raw Brazil Nut Salted Caramel Dip **98**
Dark Chocolates with Creamy Mint Filling **99**
Carrot Cake Bites Dipped in Cashew Cream Cheeze **100**
Blackberry Ice-Cream Cake with Lemon Cashew Cream Cheeze & Hemp Seed Crust **101**
Chocolate Covered Oatmeal Raisin Cookies **102**
Thick Chocolate Shake with Pumpkin Seeds **102**
Banana Split Pudding **103**
Raspberry Bars **104**

Vegan Chocolate Banana Pie

Prep+Cook Time: 15 mins

SERVES 1

2 oz hazelnuts
2 oz brazil nuts
4 tbsp rice syrup or preferred sweetener (agave, stevia)
1 tbsp coconut oil
1 ripe banana
1 tbsp cocoa powder
1 tsp ground flax seeds

1. Put the hazelnuts, brazil nuts, 3 tbsp rice syrup and the coconut oil in a food processor. Process until well ground and sticky.
2. Line a pie tin with cling film. Put the sticky mixture inside and with your fingers form a pie case. Cover with another layer of cling film and put in the freezer, preferably overnight.
3. Peel the banana. Cut it in half and cut 3 small slices for decoration. Put the rest of the banana, the cocoa powder, 1 tbsp of rice syrup and the flax seeds in the blender. Blend until you have a smooth chocolate cream.
4. Remove the pie case from the freezer. Remove the cling film. Pour the chocolate banana cream into the pie case and put in the fridge for 10 minutes to firm up. Serve with the banana slices on top.

Vegan Chocolate Orange Pie

Prep+Cook Time: 15 mins

SERVES 1

2 oz hazelnuts
2 oz brazil nuts
5 tbsp rice syrup or sweetener of choice
1 tbsp coconut oil
½ ripe avocado
2 tbsp cocoa powder
1 tbsp fresh orange juice
Orange segments for decoration

1. Put the hazelnuts, brazil nuts, 3 tbsp rice syrup and the coconut oil in a food processor. Process until well ground and sticky.

2. Line a pie tin with cling film. Put the sticky mixture inside and with your fingers form a pie case. Cover with another layer of cling film and put in the freezer, preferably overnight.

3. Put the avocado, 2 tbsp rice syrup, cocoa powder and orange juice in a blender. Blend until smooth.

4. Take the pie case out of the freezer and remove the cling film. Pour the chocolate orange mixture into the pie case. Decorate with chocolate orange segments and serve immediately.

Chocolate and Strawberry Cup

Prep+Cook Time: 15 mins

SERVES 1

½ can coconut milk
1 tbsp agave nectar
1 tsp vanilla extract
6 chocolate biscuits (approx) (check the ingredients to make sure they are vegan)
16 frozen strawberries (approx)

1. Set your glasses out on the work surface.
2. Mix half a can of coconut milk with the agave nectar and the vanilla extract.
3. Crumble the biscuits and put a small layer in the bottom of each glass.
4. Put a large strawberry on top.
5. Drizzle four teaspoons of the coconut mixture over the strawberry in each glass.
6. Add another layer of crushed biscuits this time about one whole biscuit per glass.
7. Add another strawberry layer, this time I used three strawberries in each one.
8. Pour the remaining coconut mixture into the glasses, roughly an equal amount in each glass.
9. Chill for at least 2 hours before eating.

Fruit 'n' Nut Balls

Prep+Cook Time: 15 mins

SERVES 18 balls

4 oz dried apricots – soaked for at least 2 hours
4 oz dates – pitted and soaked for at least 2 hours
2 tbsp agave nectar (optional: only necessary if you have a *really* sweet tooth)
4 oz hazelnuts
4 oz dark chocolate
1½ oz desiccated coconut

1. First make sure you have some space in your freezer. Then put the hazelnuts in a blender and blend so you get small pieces (you could also chop by hand), but don't go too far you want little crunchy bits, not a powder.
2. Take the hazelnuts out of the blender and put them in a mixing bowl. Now drain the soaking apricots and dates and put them in the blender with the agave if you are using it. Blend until smooth.
3. Put in the mixing bowl with the hazelnuts and combine. Now make little balls of the mixture. Put them on a baking tray covered in baking parchment and put them in the freezer, for about 2 hours.
4. After 2 hours they will have firmed up a bit so you can use your hands to even out the "balls". Put desiccated coconut into a clean bowl. Now melt the chocolate, in the microwave or bain marie.
5. Take each ball and drop it into the melted chocolate. Using a teaspoon (so as not to burn yourself) roll the ball in chocolate then take it out and drop it into the bowl of coconut. Roll it around again and once coated place back on the baking tray/parchment paper. Return to the freezer.
6. Once the chocolate has solidified you can take them off the baking tray and put them in tupperware in the fridge.

Homemade Chocolate Spread

Prep+Cook Time: 15 mins

SERVES 2

4 oz walnuts
4 oz hazelnuts
3 tbsp cocoa powder
1½ oz agave nectar

1. Put the nuts in a powerful blender and pulse until they become a fine powder.
2. Add cocoa powder and agave nectar and pulse again until completely mixed.
3. Store in a glass jar in the fridge.

Mint Basil Choc Chip Ice-Cream

Prep+Cook Time: 10 mins

SERVES 3

6 cup can coconut milk
¼ cup loosely packed peppermint leaves
¼ cup loosely packed basil leaves
2 tsp peppermint extract
3 tbsp agave syrup
¼ cup vegan chocolate chips

1. Put everything in a bowl except the chocolate chips and blend together with a hand blender.
2. Mix in the chocolate chips and pour into a container suitable for the freezer.
3. After four hours (it won't be fully set yet), remove from the freezer and whisk the mixture using a hand or electric whisk. Return to the freezer.
4. After another four hours, remove and whisk again. Return to the freezer.
5. Remember to take out of the freezer at least 20 minutes before serving.

Peanut Butter Truffles

Prep+Cook Time: 15 mins

SERVES 12 truffles

4 oz digestive biscuits
6 oz peanut butter
5 tbsp agave nectar
2 oz dark chocolate

1. Crush the biscuits.
2. Put the peanut butter and agave nectar in a saucepan over a very low heat and melt together, stir the whole time. When the peanut butter and agave are melted add the biscuit crumbs, remove from the heat and mix together thoroughly.
3. Form twelve balls with the mixture using your hands. Now melt the chocolate, for 1 minute in the microwave or in a bain marie over a low heat.
4. Drop the peanut butter balls, one by one, in the melted chocolate until coated.
5. Remove from the chocolate and leave to dry on greaseproof paper.

Piña Colada Chia Seed Mousse

Prep+Cook Time: 10 mins

SERVES 4

2 lb clean pineapple (topped and tailed, cored and peeled)
1½ cup coconut milk
4 tbsp agave nectar (optional, but we like the extra sweetness)
2½ oz chia seeds
Desiccated coconut to sprinkle on top

1. Blend the first four ingredients together.
2. Pour into bowls or jam jars, refrigerate overnight.
3. Remove from the fridge about 15 minutes before serving.
4. Sprinkle desiccated coconut on top and serve!

Valentine's Day Truffles

Prep+Cook Time: 10 mins

SERVES 10 truffles

2½ oz unsweetened desiccated coconut
6 tbsp cocoa powder (divided use)
1-2 tbsp strawberry jam

1. Mix coconut with 3 tablespoons of cocoa powder and 1 tbsp of jam. Mix thoroughly. It will seem impossible that this is enough jam but keep on mixing until it forms a stiff mixture.

2. Taste the mixture and if it tastes too dry or not sweet enough for you add 1 teaspoon more of jam and mix again. Repeat (shouldn't need more than 3 teaspoons of extra jam) until you are satisfied with the flavor.

3. Put 3 tablespoons of cocoa powder on a plate. With clean hands form balls a little smaller than a golf ball with the mixture and roll in cocoa powder.

4. Store in an airtight container in the fridge. I find they taste better the second day, if they last that long!

Vegan Mint Chocolate Thins

Prep+Cook Time: 20 mins

SERVES 24 chocolate thins

7 oz dark (70%) vegan chocolate
5 oz coconut cream
2 tsp mint extract
2 tbsp agave syrup

1. Place a clean chocolate mould on a flat surface in your kitchen.
2. Take half the chocolate and put it in a microwave proof bowl.
3. Melt the chocolate in the microwave. Start with 30 seconds on full power and if not melted try 10 seconds more each time until melted.
4. With a teaspoon, spoon the chocolate into the mould. You want a thin layer in the bottom of each mould.
5. Place the mould in the freezer for about half an hour.
6. Meanwhile mix the coconut cream, mint extract and agave syrup in a small bowl.
7. Remove the mould from the freezer.
8. With a teaspoon place a small amount of the mint cream in each mould.
9. Return to the freezer 30 minutes.
10. Melt the rest of the chocolate in the same way as before.
11. Remove the mould from the freezer.
12. Top the coconut cream with a layer of melted chocolate.
13. Return to the freezer for another 30 minutes.
14. Enjoy.
15. It's best to store these in the fridge, especially in warm weather.

Almond Biscuits

Prep+Cook Time: 20 mins

SERVES 20 biscuits

7 oz ground almonds
2 flax eggs (2 tbsps ground flax mixed with 6 tbsps water and left in the fridge for 15 minutes)
6 tbsp agave nectar
½ tsp cinnamon

1. Preheat the oven to 390 F.
2. Make up the flax eggs.
3. Put all the ingredients in a bowl and mix until well combined.
4. Break off little balls of mixture, flatten and place on a baking tray lined with parchment paper.
5. Bake for 9-10 minutes until golden on top.

Melting Blueberry Fudge

Prep+Cook Time: 10 mins

SERVES 2

1 c blueberries
3 oz coconut oil
½ cup organic coconut milk
4 medjool dates
1 tbsp cacao powder
2 tbsp chia seeds

1. Put all ingredients in Vitamix except chia seeds, blend until smooth. If not blending use plunger tool or add a little more coconut milk as you go.
2. Once smooth, blend in chia seeds until smooth again.
3. Transfer into small cups in mini cupcake liners or grease pan with coconut oil.
4. Set in freezer for 1 hour, remove and enjoy!

Quinoa, Carrot and Baby Marrow Cakes

Prep+Cook Time: 40 mins

SERVES 10

½ cup quinoa
4 medium sized onions, grated
12 oz grams baby marrows, grated
¾ spring onions, sliced
oregano (either dry or fresh, chopped)
salt and pepper to taste
3 very heaped tablespoons Gluten Free Tapioca Flour (cake wheat flour will work just as well)
and extra Tapioca Flour to roll cakes in before frying (cake wheat flour will work just as well)
Oil for frying

1. Cook Quinoa as per packet instructions, but using only ½ cup quinoa to 1 cup of boiling water, let simmer until done, approximately 15 minutes.
2. Grate the carrots, and set aside.
3. Slice the spring onions, and set aside
4. Grate the baby marrows. Place on a dish towel and sprinkle with salt. Let it sit awhile, the longer the better, and then squeeze the baby marrows to help draw out the water content. Be careful not to pile on the salt otherwise your veggie cakes will be overly salty.
5. Once the water is all out as best you can, place the quinoa, carrots, baby marrow, spring onions a good sprinkling of oregano, salt and pepper into a medium sized bowl.
6. Mix the ingredients until combined.
7. Then, add a heaped tablespoon of flour at a time, mixing well, after each addition.
8. Shape into balls with the help of a tablespoon.
9. Coat each ball with a little of the extra flour and set aside. (If you need more flour, to coat, just add accordingly)
10. In a large frying pan, heat up a little oil. I used vegetable oil and fry the veggie cakes until crisp and golden brown.
11. Serve with a crisp salad for a healthy lunch or with baby potatoes and vegetables for dinner. Enjoy!

Vegan Opera Slice

Prep+Cook Time: 1 hour

SERVES 6 slices

For the almond sponge:
2 oz ground almonds
1 oz extra virgin olive oil
1 tsp baking powder
1 tsp vanilla extract
2 oz agave nectar
2 rounded tbsp "no-egg"
3 tbsp water
2 tbsp wholemeal flour
   (gluten free if necessary)

For the coffee syrup:
4 oz water
1 tbsp agave nectar
2 tbsp espresso coffee

For the chocolate and coffee buttercream:
1 ripe avocado
2 tbsp espresso coffee
1 tsp vanilla extract
4 tbsp agave nectar
1 tbsp cocoa powder

For the topping:
5 oz dark chocolate

1. Preheat the oven to 350 F. Line a baking tray with baking parchment (size: 12 1/2" x 8 1/2").
2. Put all the ingredients for the almond sponge except the no-egg and the water, in a bowl and mix together. You can do this by hand.
3. Put the no-egg and water in a separate bowl and whisk with an electric whisk until the no-egg mixture looks like egg whites that have been beaten until stiff.
4. Fold the no-egg whites into the almond mixture with a metal spoon.
5. Put the mixture in the baking tray and use a spatula to push the mix right into the corners. This will form a very thin layer over the baking tray. Definitely not more than ½ inch thick.
6. Put in the oven until the mixture is set and golden. About 10 minutes.
7. Take the almond sponge out of the oven and leave to cool. Do not remove the parchment paper from the cake before it's cool or it will disintegrate.
8. While the sponge is cooling make the other components. For the buttercream put all the ingredients in a blender and blend until smooth.
9. Make the coffee syrup. Boil the water and agave syrup until the amount of water is reduced by about half. Remove from the

heat and leave to cool. When cool add the coffee.

10. Putting the cake together. Cut the almond sponge in half. Place one half on a plate.
11. With a pastry brush, brush the sponge with coffee syrup.
12. With a spatula, spread half the buttercream on the sponge.
13. Melt half the dark chocolate in the microwave. (about 1 minute) Pour on top of the buttercream and spread with the spatula.
14. Put the next layer of cake on.
15. Repeat the layers. Coffee syrup, buttercream, dark chocolate.
16. Leave to cool, first at room temperature, then in the fridge.
17. If you wish you can neaten up the edges by trimming them. Warm the blade of the knife under the hot tap. Quickly dry the knife and cut off the edges. The warm knife will melt the chocolate so you can cut it. Please be careful with sharp knives and hot water!
18. Enjoy. Keep leftovers in the fridge.

Strawberry Chocolate Vegan Cheesecake

Prep+Cook Time: 30 mins

SERVES 4

For the Base:
5 prunes
2 oz walnuts

For the chocolate layer
2 small avocados
2 tbsp cocoa powder
2 tbsp agave syrup
1 tsp vanilla extract
1 tbsp coconut oil in liquid state

For the "cheese" layer
5 oz / 1 cup raw cashews
3 tbsp agave nectar
1 tsp vanilla extract
1 tbsp coconut oil in liquid state
2 strawberries

1. Put the cashews to soak in water at least 8 hours.
2. Put the prunes to soak about 30 minutes.
3. Put the walnuts in a blender and pulse to get finely chopped walnuts.
4. Drain the prunes and remove the stones, if they have them still in, add to the blender with the walnuts and pulse until you have some sticky goo.
5. Line your cake tins with plenty of cling film, you want enough to cover the whole cake when you are finished.
6. Put the walnut and prune mixture in the cake tins and spread out with a teaspoon to make a thin layer that goes right up to the edges.
7. Put the cake tins in the freezer for at least 2 hours.
8. Put all the ingredients for the chocolate layer in the blender and mix well.
9. Take the cake tins out of the freezer, add the chocolate layer spreading it out with the back of a teaspoon so that it reaches the edges.
10. Put in the freezer for at least two hours.
11. Wash and hull the strawberries.
12. Cut into slices.
13. Choose a slice to cut a heart out of and set aside.

14. Place all the ingredients for the "cheese" layer except the strawberries in a blender and blend until smooth.
15. Take the cake tins out of the freezer.
16. Scatter the sliced strawberries over the chocolate layer.
17. Add the cheese layer on top, smoothing it with the back of a teaspoon as you did with the other layers.
18. Top with your heart-shaped strawberry and cover with the cling film so you don't get ice crystals in the cake.
19. Return to the freezer for another 2 hours at least.
20. Remove from the freezer 1 hour before serving. Take cake out of pan and remove clingfilm while cake is still firm from the freezer.

Brownie With Avocado Choco Icing & Kiwi Gummies

Prep+Cook Time: 30 mins

SERVES 2

Kiwi Gummies:
2 Kiwis, peeled

Choco Avo Icing:
1 avocado, pitted and peeled
3 tbsp cacao powder
1 tbsp coconut nectar (raw) or maple syrup (not raw)

Raw Brownie Squares:
1 cup pecan
1 cup rolled oats
2 tbsp coconut nectar
2 tbsp cacao powder

1. Peel and slice kiwi.
2. Place on mesh dehydrator tray with brownie and dry for equal amount of time.
3. Put all ingredients in food processor, mix on high until smooth.
4. Ice brownies once dehydrated, top with kiwi. Do not wait to eat, avocado goes bad quickly and will taste too much like avocado as a result. Store in fridge if you must.
5. Put nuts in food processor, mix until slightly larger than grain of sand.
6. Add in remaining ingredients and process on high until everything sticks.
7. Transfer mixture to a rectangle or square shaped pan. Press firmly into shape. You will use this to get the square brownie shape.
8. Place pan upside down on mesh dehydrator tray and shake or pat on bottom of pan until brownie falls out in full shape.
9. Using a dehydrator, dry at 275 F for 1 hour.

Choco Chip Cookie Bites

Prep+Cook Time: 1 hour 10 mins

SERVES 10-15

1 cup gluten-free rolled oats
2 medjool dates
1 banana, ripe
1 tbsp coconut nectar (raw) or maple syrup (not raw)
3 tbsp coconut oil
½ cup coconut flour
½ cup hemp seeds
¼ cup cacao nibs

1. Put all ingredients in food processor except for hemp seeds and cacao nibs. Mix on high until formed into large solid ball of dough.
2. Transfer cookie dough into large bowl and mix in hemp seeds and cacao nibs by hand.
3. Roll cookie into small round dough balls, flatten each ball slightly. Place on mesh dehydrator tray.
4. Using a dehydrator, dry cookies at 250 F for 1 hour. Should remain moist inside.

Apple Stacks with Raw Brazil Nut Salted Caramel Dip

Prep+Cook Time: 30 mins

SERVES 2

½ cup golden berries, dried & soaked
3 medjool dates, pitted
¼ c brazil nuts, soaked
½ lemon, squeezed
1 tsp himalayan salt
2 tbsp coconut nectar (raw) or maple syrup (not raw)

Toppings:
Whatever you would like!
Banana, nuts, seeds, cacao nibs

1. Soak dried golden berries, dates, and brazil nuts in a large bowl filled with water for 2-4 hours (the longer the better).
2. Once soaking is complete, put all ingredients into Vitamix or high speed blender and blend until smooth. Apply to anything and enjoy!

Dark Chocolates with Creamy Mint Filling

Prep+Cook Time: 40 mins

SERVES 10-15

Creamy Mint Filling:
1 cup cashews
1 lemon, squeezed
¼ cup coconut milk
2 tbsp coconut nectar (raw)
    or maple syrup (not raw)
6 fresh mint leaves
2 cup coconut, shredded
½ tsp peppermint extract

Chocolate:
½ cup dark choco
1 tbsp coconut oil

1. Put coconut in food processor, mix on high for 2 minutes.
2. Put remaining ingredients into Vitamix, blend until smooth.
3. Transfer ingredients from Vitamix to food processor, mix again until fully combined.
4. Roll mixture into 10 – 15 small balls and place on parchment on plate in freezer for 10 minutes.
5. Melt chocolate and coconut oil in small pot on low heat until smooth. Remove from heat.
6. Remove mint balls from freezer and using a spoon or fork dip into chocolate. Once fully covered set back on parchment and repeat until each one is coated.
7. Place in freezer for 10 – 20 minutes then enjoy!

Carrot Cake Bites Dipped in Cashew Cream Cheeze

Prep+Cook Time: 1 hour 15 mins

SERVES 15 balls

Raw Carrot Cake Bites:
2 cup carrots, shredded or leftover from juicing
1 cup coconut flour or oat flour
1 cup figs or medjool dates, pitted
1 tsp cinnamon
½ tsp nutmeg
½ tsp vanilla extract
2 tbsp coconut nectar (raw) or maple syrup (not raw)

Additions:
Mix in raisin, walnuts, pecans, dried cranberries, be creative!

Cashew Cream Cheeze:
1 cup cashews, soaked if you can
2 tbsp maple syrup
½ lemon, squeezed
2 tbsp coconut oil

1. Juice carrots and set pulp aside OR finely chop carrots and set aside.
2. In food processor, mix figs or dates on high until smooth. Add coconut nectar/maple syrup and blend again on high.
3. Add other ingredients and mix until smooth. Transfer to large bowl and set aside.
4. Mix in additions. Once complete, roll mixture into small balls and place on mesh dehydrator tray.
5. Using a dehydrator, dry at 250 F for 1 – 2 hours, depending on how soft you like the cake to be.
6. Put Cashew Cream Cheeze ingredients into Vitamix and blend on high until smooth.

Blackberry Ice-Cream Cake with Lemon Cashew Cream Cheeze & Hemp Seed Crust

Prep+Cook Time: 30 mins

SERVES 2

Hemp Seed Crust:
½ cup hemp seeds
½ cup medjool dates, pitted

Ice-Cream Cake:
1 banana
1 cup blackberries

Cashew Cream Cheeze Frosting:
1 cup cashews, soaked if you can
2 tbsp maple syrup
½ lemon, squeezed
2 tbsp coconut oil

Topping:
Hemp seeds
Crushed blackberries

1. In a food processor, mix seed crust until sticks in one large ball. Press firmly into small round pan (4 x 4 inches) that has been greased with coconut oil for easy remove. Set in freezer.
2. In a Vitamix or high speed blender, mix ice-cream cake until smooth. Transfer into another round pan of equal size or top crust and put back into freezer.
3. Put frosting ingredients into Vitamix and blend until smooth.
4. Remove crust and ice-cream from freezer. Run bottom of pan under hot water for 30 seconds then transfer to plate.
5. Ice the cake with frosting and add toppings. Enjoy!

Chocolate Covered Oatmeal Raisin Cookies

Prep+Cook Time: 30 mins

SERVES 2

1 c oats
¾ c almond butter or any nut/seed butter
1 tsp cinnamon
2 tbsp maple syrup (not raw) or coconut nectar (raw)
½ c raisins

1. Put all ingredients except for raisins in food processor and mix on high until combined. Transfer to large bowl.
2. Mix in raisins in large bowl.
3. Roll cookie dough into medium sized balls and place on mesh dehydrator tray.
4. Using a dehydrator, dry at 250 F for 1 hour.
5. Remove from dehydrator once dry and dip into chocolate from this recipe. Place on plate and refrigerate for 20 minutes.

Thick Chocolate Shake with Pumpkin Seeds

Prep+Cook Time: 5 mins

SERVES 1

2 bananas
½ cup pineapple
3 tbsp pumpkin seeds
½ cup almond milk or coconut milk
2 tbsp chia seeds
2 tbsp cacao powder

1. Put all ingredients in Vitamix and blend until smooth. Now enjoy!

Banana Split Pudding

Prep+Cook Time: 10 mins

SERVES 2

Coconut Whipped:
1 can organic coconut milk, unflavored & unsweetened
1 tsp vanilla extract
1 tbsp coconut nectar (raw) or maple syrup (not raw)
4 tbsp coconut flour

Banana Pudding:
2 bananas
1 cup coconut milk
1 cup cashews, soaked
2 tbsp coconut nectar (raw) or maple syrup (not raw)

Additions:
Vegan dark chocolate chips

1. Use thick, clear liquid portion of coconut milk (should be separated when you open the can). Set aside less dense white coconut milk for banana pudding. Blend coconut whipped ingredients in a Vitamix on high until smooth and creamy. Set aside in small bowl.

2. Using Vitamix for a second round, blend banana pudding on high until smooth.

3. Mix pudding with coconut whipped and add in dark chocolate chips. Enjoy!

Raspberry Bars

Prep+Cook Time: 20 mins

SERVES 5

Bars:
1 cup walnuts
1 cup dried coconut
1 tsp vanilla extract
½ tsp cinnamon
½ cup medjool dates, pitted
1 tbsp coconut oil
Pinch of sea salt

Topping:
1 cup raspberries
2 tbsp chia seeds
¼ cup coconut sugar

1. Combine bars ingredients into food processor, mix on high. Set aside a small amount for topping crumble. Place in small rectangle pan, flatten and set aside.

2. Combine topping ingredients in food processor, mix on high. Layer on top of bars. Add crumble.

3. Freeze bars for 10 minutes. Remove from cold, slice and enjoy!

4. Sauces, Pâtés and Dips

Cashew Nut Cheese with Sundried Tomatoes **106**
Chestnut and Sundried Tomato Pâté **106**
Carrot, Sundried Tomato and Pecan Sauce **107**

Spaghetti with Classic Pesto (almost) **108**
Sundried Tomato Sauce **109**
Sweet Pesto **109**
Tangy Green Salad Dressing **110**

Cashew Nut Cheese with Sundried Tomatoes

Prep+Cook Time: 35 mins

SERVES 5

2 oz raw cashews, soaked (preferably overnight), drained and rinsed
2 tbsp lemon juice
1 tbsp extra virgin olive oil
1 tbsp water
6 sundried tomatoes, soaked (about 15 minutes) and drained
1 tsp garlic powder
½ tsp salt

1. Preheat the oven to 350 F.
2. Put al the ingredients for the cheese into a blender and blend for a good 5 minutes until everything is a paste.
3. Put into an oiled ramekin and bake for 30 minutes.
4. Allow to cool before taking out of the ramekin. It's really that easy!

Chestnut and Sundried Tomato Pâté

Prep+Cook Time: 20 mins

SERVES 4

4 oz cooked peeled chestnuts (the ones that come in a vacuum pack)
8 sundried tomatoes
2 tbsp extra virgin olive oil
Pinch of salt

1. Soak the sundried tomatoes in boiling water for 15 minutes.
2. Drain.
3. Put all the ingredients in a blender and blend until smooth.

Carrot, Sundried Tomato and Pecan Sauce

Prep+Cook Time: 35 mins

SERVES 4

2 oz pecans – soaked in water for at least 2 hours
4 carrots
2 tbsp nutritional yeast
2 oz water – filtered or mineral
1½ tbsp tamari
1½ tbsp lime juice
1 tsp sea salt
3 sundried tomatoes

1. Peel the carrots but don't top and tail them yet.
2. Steam or boil them for 20 minutes until soft. Meanwhile drain and rinse the pecans and blend them with the water until smooth.
3. When the carrots are done, cut off the ends and add them to the bowl with the pecans and water. Add all the other ingredients except the sundried tomatoes and blend to make a thick sauce. Taste to see if you need more salt.
4. Chop the sundried tomatoes finely and add to the sauce.
5. Allow to sit in the fridge so the flavor can develop if possible.
6. Enjoy with your favorite salad. You can also blend the tomatoes in with the rest of the ingredients – it's up to you!

Spaghetti with Classic Pesto (almost)

Prep+Cook Time: 25 mins

SERVES 2

4 oz wholewheat spaghetti
2 small potatoes
4 green french beans or a 6 courgette batons about 4 inch long (basically bean shaped)
½ oz basil leaves
2 tbsp pine nuts
½ a large clove of garlic Or 1 small one
2 tbsp nutritional yeast
3 tbsp extra virgin olive oil
Salt

1. Put a large saucepan filled with water on the stove to boil.
2. Cut the potatoes into chunks (leave the skin on) and add to the saucepan.
3. Wash the beans, top and tail them and cut them into 3 equal parts OR wash the courgette and cut it into bean sized pieces.
4. Put the basil leaves, pine nuts, garlic, a generous pinch of salt, nutritional yeast and olive oil in a blender and blend until smooth.
5. When the water is boiling add a pinch of salt, a dash of olive oil, the spaghetti and the beans or courgette. Leave to boil for 10 minutes or according to the cooking instructions for the spaghetti.
6. Place the serving dishes on the counter. Add three tablespoons of cooking water to each dish. Drain the spaghetti (and beans/courgette and potato). Put the spaghetti, beans/courgette and potatoes on the plates. Add the pesto on top and mix thoroughly. Sprinkle with more nutritional yeast if desired.

Sundried Tomato Sauce

Prep+Cook Time: 20 mins

SERVES 4

7 oz cream (dairy or vegetable is fine I especially like oat cream)
6 sundried tomatoes
1 inch leek (white part only)
Half an onion
1 tbsp extra virgin olive oil
Salt to taste

1. Put the sundried tomatoes in water to rehydrate if the a dried or remove the excess oil with kitchen paper if they are in oil.
2. Chop the onion and leek and sauté in the olive oil with a pinch of salt for 5 minutes. Put everything (cooked onion and leek, cream and sundried tomatoes) in a hand blender and mix until completely smooth.
3. Taste to see if you need to add more salt. Return to the pan and heat through.
4. Serve.

Sweet Pesto

Prep+Cook Time: 5 mins

SERVES 4

1 oz mint leaves
25 raw pistachios
3 tbsp agave nectar
A squeeze of lemon juice
Lemon zest
Fruit or ice-cream to serve

1. Blend all the ingredients except the lemon zest in a blender.
2. Serve with fruit or ice-cream.
3. Top with lemon zest.

Tangy Green Salad Dressing

Prep+Cook Time: 5 mins

SERVES 1

1 spring onion (Scallion) white part only
½ cup flat leaf parsley
2 tbsp tahini
1 tbsp water
Juice of half a lemon
Salt to taste

1. Wash the parsley and remove the stems.
2. Roughly chop the spring onion.
3. Blend all the ingredients with a hand blender until smooth.

5. Drinks / Smoothies

Mango, Beetroot and Cherry
　Smoothie **112**
Flat Peach and Loquat
　Smoothie **112**

Caramel Apple Shake **113**
Celery Lemonade **113**

Mango, Beetroot and Cherry Smoothie

Prep+Cook Time: 20 mins

SERVES 2

1 beetroot, washed and peeled
1 mango, peeled and stoned
10 cherries, washed and stoned
A squeeze of lime juice
4 crushed pistachios

1. Put all the ingredients except the pistachios into a blender and blend until smooth.
2. Pour into glasses and sprinkle the crushed pistachios on top.
3. Cheers and have a great weekend everyone!

Flat Peach and Loquat Smoothie

Prep+Cook Time: 5 mins

SERVES 1

3 flat peaches
2 loquats
1 orange zest only

1. Wash the orange and remove the zest. If you have a zester leave it as it is. If you don't have a zester use a vegetable peeler, being careful not to get the white bitter part, then slice the zest into thin strips with a knife.
2. Peel and stone the flat peaches and loquats.
3. Put the fruit in a blender until smooth.
4. Serve sprinkled with the orange zest.

Caramel Apple Shake

Prep+Cook Time: 5 mins

SERVES 1

3 red apples, cored
1 cup almond milk
1 tsp cinnamon
½ tsp vanilla
1 lime, squeezed
1 tbsp blackstrap molasses
2 tbsp almond butter

1. Using a Vitamix, blend apples, almond milk, and vanilla extract until smooth. Pour into large glass.
2. In a small bowl, mix lime juice, molasses, and almond butter. Stir into apple shake and enjoy!

Celery Lemonade

Prep+Cook Time: 5 mins

SERVES 1

10 stalks of celery
2 cucumber
2 lemons
Parsley (optional)

1. Juice all ingredients in Juicer and enjoy!

Measurement Conversions

Volume Equivalents (Liquid)

US Standart	Ounces	Metric (approx.)
2 tbsp	1 fl oz	30 ml
¼ cup	2 fl oz	60 ml
½ cup	4 fl oz	120 ml
1 cup	8 fl oz	240 ml
1½ cups	12 fl oz	355 ml
2 cups (1 pint)	16 fl oz	475 ml
4 cups (1 quart)	32 fl oz	1 L
1 gallon	128 fl oz	4 L

Oven Temperatures

Fahrenheit (F)	Celsius (C) (approx.)
250 F	120 C
300 F	150 C
325 F	165 C
350 F	180 C
375 F	190 C
400 F	200 C
425 F	220 C
450 F	230 C

Volume Equivalents (Dry)

US Standart	Metric (approx.)
¼ tsp	1 ml
½ tsp	2 ml
¾ tsp	4 ml
1 tsp	5 ml
1 tbsp	15 ml
¼ cup	59 ml
½ cup	118 ml
¾ cup	177 ml
1 cup	235 ml
2 cups (1 pint)	475 ml
4 cups (1 quart)	1 L

Weight Equivalents

US Standart	Metric (approx.)
½ oz	15 g
1 oz	30 g
2 oz	60 g
4 oz	115 g
8 oz	225 g
12 oz	340 g
16 oz (1 lbs)	455 g

Made in the USA
Columbia, SC
14 April 2020